COOLER THAN
OCTOBER SUNLIGHT

COOLER THAN OCTOBER SUNLIGHT

Selected Poems *1959 - 2014*

J I M   L E V Y

Levy, Jim, 1940-

ISBN: 0692366210
ISBN 13: 9780692366219

First edition

Atalaya Press

for Phaedra, Alexander and Sara
who have sustained me

and for Harvey S. Mudd
who has inspired me
for over half a century

PREFACE

These poems were written over a span of fifty-five years, from 1959 to 2014. They are more or less chronological. In 1971 I threw away four novels, some stories and many poems, discouraged by the quality of what I had written up to then. I again threw away many poems, along with some essays and stories, in 1985. The early poems which appear in this book were recovered from letters to friends and relatives or from journals. After 1985, I kept almost everything that I wrote.

I have never thought of myself as a professional writer but I have almost always been writing. My mother was an avid reader and hoped to be a writer, but at her death, we did not find anything written by her. I think that my writing is a fulfillment of her dream.

A biography appears at the back of this book which I hope will put some of the poems into context.

POEMS

In these times of solitude, when under the lemon trees
the insects are furious in the grass
and the whole great world is held mute
and still and solemn in my soul,
the fear of life makes life a tremulous act,
my softly beating blood makes afternoons eternities

. . . long days of sleeping in the grass, waking,
drifting into states between

. . . the streaks of light and the blind thick lemons
and me adrift and bewildered on a crumbling sea.

Upland, California 1959

Looking across water
I see a stream of cars
glittering on the bridge.
I see ships in dock and tiny workers.

I have suffered
and come through suffering.
Why does it have to be solitary?
Why do I choose a solitary joy?

I feel faint with lust.
I feel giddy, sick with desire;
yet I am pure and solitary,
chaste as a hermit and frugal with myself.
I am Lazarus, come forth,
a young man, come forth,
yet shrunken inward
despite God's gift,
with God's gift.

I am caught before
I know I am sought
and dragged down the lanes of pain,
am caught, stunned silly,
caught and killed.
Thus you, crack shot,
shoot me down,
and dying, I plunder downwards,
rich in death, and greedy.

I plunge into the wet night
as if in a rage –
really I just want to be alone.

I head for the bay
not knowing how far I will go.
The wet trees are beautiful
shining above the streetlights.

Between the trees, the distant city
glimmers in the rain.

I don't like what I must do,
turn back, be less than myself, and more.

She said to me
"of course I'll go
but wed – no.
Of course I'll love
but buy you, tie you, no."

She said, "nothing lasts,
nothing changes, that's the truth.
The whole long past awaits us.
That's the mirth.
That's the curse
that nothing lasts,
not the birds or boredom
not the past or past deceptions,
not the life or death I led.
I'll go, but where, who knows?
I'll go, with you, but who are we?"

I burn but paradoxically
for paradoxically I am not.
In the hills the shining husks
of oats and barley burn,
the husks from which the seeds
have slipped like drifts of snow.

Hearing my heart
beating so loudly,
hearing the world's
beating so darkly,
how is it that such a void is?
And is so painfully?

The Horseshoer's Wife
"When he is finished with it
he lets it loose and takes another
from the five still tied to the fence.
He'll nudge her if she doesn't stand
and if she turns and nips
he'll smack her across the face.
He clicks his hammer twice
twice against the iron
then strikes the shoe.
His arm is red, the bicep white.
Last night he hit me with his fist.
He is mild the way he hammers out the world
the way he wants it."

What are the things that when I see them
my soul catches its breath and rocks faster?
In Italy it was long paths seen from the trains
stretching across fields,
long worn shining ribbons of earth.
But where would I walk?

Then in Topanga it was a workshop
where a man's tools were racked,
hammers and files and saws lodged on the wall,
nails sorted in bins by size.
But what would I build?
What do I feel is not built?

Now in Sonoma it is a fallen tree
with its white branches oscillating
between the splayed limbs of a girl
and the whitening bones of a beast.
I wonder where I have been
and where we are going.

The beginning
I was seeking an explanation which would reveal to me the secret of life
and I discovered that life has no secret.
Here is life exactly as it appears to be.

The journey
As soon as I realized that life make no sense whatsoever,
it began to make sense.
It was at that point that I became really confused.

The end
Occasionally a star or a stone speaks to me of love and eternity.

In Mexico

Long dark boats lifting their nostrils in the air
and dancing slowly on the waves
the squalor of the husky bells rasps
in the womb of the morning
women selling coconuts, candies, spoons bananas
flags peanuts rings mangos
men stream by selling idols pants chairs
and tins and apples strawberries
Superhombres petroleo and knives
dishcloths shirts CineVidas flowers sombreros.
Diesel fumes and shit fill the air.
In the markets peaches, apples
tomatoes papayas meat fish,
tongue hoof and hide, fried fat.
Cries: helados! agua! leche! manzanas!
Cries: Agua! Leche! Manzana! Muerte!
White metallic sunlight blazes through the faded garden.
Butterflies tatter the plaza roses
that are burning with a thin and lacquered flame.
Locust rattle, trains travel twenty feet
balloons hang like wrinkled scrotum from the arbors
empty tres equis bottles tumble down the empty street.
All night the roses lick the air.

The rains come
first a whisper on corn leaves
on tiles, whispers and sighs.
The large empty room fills with thunder and white light.
The bedstead gleams.
Then on the roof, passionate drumming of rain.

A man rises and in a spurt of rage
glares at the mirror which reflects nothing.

Dark Mexico.
It is always dark here
English cannot say it
No language can say it
It is not speakable
It is not silence
It is a roar without language
an empty scream
a shriek that has gone on so long no one hears it.
Sleep is like death, they say,
but not the sleep here, not this death,
they do not resemble each other.
Sleep is troubled, they say
and death is absolute
but here it is sleep that is absolute
and death is wide awake.

We are sensualists, thinkers, mystics, cuckolds, dreamers, actors
who are united in spirit and alone in the flesh
– you are old when you know that or the other way around.
We cry, holler, sing and bleat. We ask all questions and answer none.
If we could answer one, just one, on any topic,
we would be able to answer them all.
We are free to abstain from answering any of them
but not from asking them.

I choose the backwater over the mainstream,
the lineaments over the heart.
I think of life as a neglected garden of lime trees
open to the street where pigs clatter by every morning.
The spirit is a garden within walls, within a bower,
and within the bower, a rose, a folded rose – wherein lies what? – eternity.

I choose life

Glorious is the risk.

The world has a serene and un-guessable logic.
We learn as we go using caresses, fists, winks and food
and do the best we can. We get a feel for the way things are,
the way things shape up, what life is.
Time, space, God, good, life and death are abstractions to a young person,
but living realities to an old person.
No one has lived more than that old woman there,
the one walking down 7th Street
behind her oxen composing an opera on her shield.
No one has lived more than that old man
who is learning to be on an equal footing with sunlight and death.
They are no longer content with running against the grain.

Words are seals to be broken, every egg and snowflake is a world,
every road a revelation, every house a dream state,
every lip a sign or signal,
every bee a garden, every hammer an anvil.
A mask is naked fear and nakedness is nothing.
Apples are feet and horror is a kind of fascination,
all that is is heel, scales, rubies,
flux, core, sun, air, dusk and dark.
From the center and source, infinities flow and form a rim of gardens,
lips, barflies, dragons, shanks, ozone, Kali and lust (dust)
pus, czar, zero, sea, Sassak, lye trigger tiger cobalt broken brass
haunt oak, Melville, the fall, daybreak,
seals, ghosts, snakes, lilies, whorls;
and each one of these is a center and a source
from which flow infinities and form rims
of wrinkled yellow apples, agate eyes, limbs, smoke,
skies, Mrs. Prentice, the 26th of May, lice twigs
"the porthole had the appearance of a horse's eye"

I'm greedy, greedy for more, for both, for everything.
Give me liberty and death.
Why should I give up my teeth,
pomegranates and all the amorous art of India
when I can have them and spirit too?

The body is greedy, the spirit is greedy. I am greedy.
What I want, simply, is speckled light, muddy water,
light flesh, the dark day, dirty crystal, the shattered word,
the ancient babe, the original likeness.
I want it all, bit by bit. I want to go down the road taking it all with me
top-heavy, lopsided, serene (even that, why not?)

striking myself against everything I encounter
and seeing my way by the sparks.

There is always confusion in our perception of the nature of things
the nature of nothing and the erotic relationship between the two.
Every apple and planet partakes of both, every fire and goat and egg.
Heaven and hell are everywhere, in the large and small,
light mixes with dark, spirit mixing with chaos,
drunkenness is a form of sobriety, father's word and mother's touch,
seven mysteries and the three laws of thermodynamics,
everything contains its opposite and everything else, all the time, always.
The things that lift us drown us.

> *"The eye with which I see God*
> *is the same as that with which he sees me."*
> *Meister Eckhart.*

Lie in the sunshine, look at the stars,
start a garden ...

egg
porch
night
mask
road
bells
dream
gate
tomorrow
taproot – like a radish
the spin

The emptiness out there, the emptiness in here
coals lanes kitchens carnivals sparks
cow dragonfly quinces noon oak, galaxy teeth fuel,
I am fuel for this fire
apple
blue syntax song
I love things, just things, themselves, without extension or essence.
I have a faith in these two oranges, in the virtue of these two oranges,
in the virtue of their existence.
Everything fascinates me, not just sunlight and footfalls
$E=mc2$
and cancer

chromosomes
John Baptist
women in plain brown wrappers

Clamorsilence
bloom bird rooftop, the dance,
ice grapes birth
last night
racks low-tide
naked
code

World, you are so beautiful. I fell in love with you
thinking you could give me what I wanted.
World, bathing naked before me,
wrap your powerful arms around my neck.
Your eyes are wide and colorless.

I see
your face
in fire
O salt
O salt

The sun is falling through the window lighting up the page
as I write the words
lupin, rose,
stars oaks grasses like green fire,
white marble of buildings,
graveheads girls rivers

snow collects on the north side of walls

Each kiss a thud, a thump on the back, a sneer.
Her lips are white.
The day is a bright empty roar.

The beauty of the unique being
naked

the sea stark
the earth round
the ridge a shark fin

the mineral sun consumes the maniac
breast-stroking in the dawn

the wounded waves pound
Nineveh and Philadelphia

the earth blown clean of dirt
the last face waving from the window of the sea

the enormous movement thinks
and carries us, whipping, left to right . . .

The night crackles now.
Listen. Do you hear trembling generation
of the snake and frog and turtle?
I can smell the generation coming. I can smell it craving.
The stars are flashing green, the marsh is drawing down the starlight.
I would be fine and sharp and finished.
I would die, be finished off.
One fine stroke
One death suffices

The best moments are the ones that catch us by surprise,
the sudden kiss, the clear thought, Saturday afternoon spent in a bar,
a walk on the docks at dawn.
Happiness is always sensual,
even mystical and intellectual convolutions,
like Jacob Boehme's or Blake's, are orgies of the senses.
Even Lao Tzu – sparse, refined orgy, an orgy of the higher senses.
The center, the still-point, is sensually alive.
It isn't static, pure or ineffable.
It's a glowing face, a laugh, a wrist, a chestnut tree,
it's everywhere all the time.
A human is a small thing but large, as in Brueghel's paintings
where people are dots, little grim brushstrokes
but possessed of a subtle dignity: a man chasing his cap,
a woman carrying a bucket of water, a child rolling dice
– the most humble acts exulted.
Even Christ carrying the cross is a tiny figure
lost in the crowd. The gospel according to Pieter Brueghel.

After doing nightmare scenes of hell, imitations of Bosch,
Brueghel painted scenes of rural life,
heaven and hell in a plowed field,
a horse, the eye of a horse, the reflection in the eye,
the reflection of a house,
the door open to the sunlit air,
a woman is sitting in the doorway knitting,
her needle is flashing signals to her lover, the butcher
who is slaughtering male calves.

In the evening my acts become rituals. Heating water for coffee,
stirring the fire are holy rites performed under the eyes of the stars.
Quiet joy permeates me.
I am soft and sexual towards the spoon and the chair.
Late at night, when she and the kids are cocooned in their beds,
I sit at the table with white paper. There seems to be a relationship
between their sleep and my wakefulness.
Their dreams support my wakefulness
and my wakefulness shelters their sleep.
They are like larvae, vulnerable and poor, the mysteries of the universe
descending upon them in the shape of dreams.

A drowsy fever rocks me.
I dream that after six years, my father and I are walking across a field
where red cattle are standing in the sunlight.
On his polished hands, the smell of garlic from the salad.

I am crossing a square
which is covered with trolley tracks like bright snail trails.
An invisible train is passing, its passage marked
only by the flashes of sparks in the wires overhead.
It rounds the corner, there is a splash of blue electricity,
and it disappears down between the hotels.
The hotels, a long row of them on either side, are old and dirty,
made of crumbling brick and rotting rods.
Their signs: Crested Hotel, Central Hotel, Hotel Savoy,
a vista of discrete doorways, a flight of stairs, a dark landing.
No Cooking in the Rooms, Absolutely No Hotplates.
No Visitors after 10 P.M. No Credit.

A man in the dark holds a stone in one hand,
a stone in the other, and strikes them together.
This is it! Seventy years or seconds.

We went there together, where we imagined, and went on,
and we parted company beyond the Pleiades somewhere
and I saw a far star faintly and something said to me That is home.
I was amazed and wanted to go there and I went, pulled by light,
and I thought That is where I started
and headed back
and I reached the sun and then the earth
and we took up again, with new names,
and journeyed out again.

Why does the memory of the light
in San Francisco move me so much?
The cool air and the sunlight
and your freckled skin.

We stopped to examine the fish
the Korean caught
and threw into a bucket.

Goodbye to all that
bloodshed and shore.

I put on my glasses
and see nothing.

Some kisses last forever
but not love.

I am surprised
how private destiny is.
I should have guessed.
Love reveals the ironies.

To gain access to her
I had to show an interest
in something beyond sex,
something like fidelity
or fate. When we danced
her steps dogged mine.
She loved more selectively
and longer.
As I loved her, she loved me more.
She loved, I left
and I was lost without her.

Yet lost myself when with her.
I loved her love of me
yet fled for a wilder rose
who knew the interplay
of lust and love and death in me.
Is there a sleight of hand here?
If I had stayed,
what would she have done with me?
To me?

"**A**nd there it is:
the act of leaving is exhilarating.
It is my weakness.
I love to leave.
Its lure is strong.

Passing towns and prairies,
trucks at crossings, 24 hour diners,
escaping all that is finished.
It's the leaving that attracts me,
not the arrival
or the illusion of a future.
Failing is part of the allure."

So I said, fleeing one woman
to another and her child,
without the possibility of ever leaving.

Outside of town with my thumb out
the good folk of Lubbock on the way to church
stared at me and the young shot the peace sign
and shouted Go Back to Moscow.

All morning in the bleak Sunday sunshine
without a ride until a man in a pickup stopped,
a Cherokee who talked about having worked for Safeway
for twenty-five years and how his Labrador
leaps and points in midair and can hold an egg
in his mouth without breaking it
and about his father Pop's balls were scrapped of gangrene
and his stepson Royce
who is tall and thin and wears thick glasses
(like mine I think) and when a thug said
"I hear you're tough you ain't so tough come down to the fairgrounds
in an hour and I'll wup your fucking ass"
Royce said not a word,
drove down there in his "charged"
and skidded through the gate and sixty feet beyond
and wearing his white shorts and steel-toed machinist boots
beat up four men.

The Cherokee's name was Scotty and he talked nonstop like this:
"Pops had this fucking mare and all he had to do was let her smell
his motherfucking hat and throw it down on the fucking ground . . ."
and so on

He was an orphan and brought up in a Home
where the custodians beat him until he ran away
at fourteen and joined the Army by paying a wino two dollars
to say "I am his father and he IS seventeen"
and fought at Salerno and Anzio.
I know Anzio, I muttered but Scotty said
the fucking I-talians were horseshit cowards
who ran fucking away.

There were certain flaws in Scotty's stories
that made me think he was making them up,
but there were details that seemed to confirm it all.
He may have been telling the truth
or more likely he himself no longer knew.
I didn't care as long as we got to Amarillo before dark.

It rained so hard it was black
so hard we couldn't hear the words
to the song on the radio

love –
        I ran
to New Orleans to lie in the dark
and ponder what love we had and lost,
what sorrow drove us to this impasse.

Not there last night,
the Mar Egeo is in port this morning.

We used to walk – remember
on the beach
and when the wind rose
we built a shack from driftwood,
three sides of weathered planks
open in the front like your dress
and I got aroused and took you
who were more than willing,
took you and me both
to beyond time and place
and we woke to the surf pounding on the shore.

Rambling out of Berkeley racing in my little Ford
past working class Richmond through Vallejo,
then over the top of the bay
and turning north towards Sonoma
with red-winged blackbirds darting in the reeds,
happy in love singing Ticket To Ride
at the top of my lungs.
Can a year have a particular beat?
How convey the motion of the Ford
and my heart and how lightly she moved
and my love. She was true. I too.

I woke up without hope
and walked out into the wide fields
and saw what may have been a river
or a layer of low mist
and still without hope or anything to do
I was happy.

Bolgatanga, Ghana 1971

Syntaxis

There is a message in the pattern of a flight
of swallows and the creases in the hand,
women shifting grains in the quarries of the teacup,
tiny bones upon a cloth, readings over viscera and dreams,
stripes on seeds, speckles on an egg, the flows
of fish and snakes and birds and spiders that defy the air.
There is meaning in the pulse fire paints upon the wall.

We listen to the voice of voiceless things:
the enunciation of my mother's hands,
the utterance of careful hair. The table has a tongue,
the walls a patterned speech. Outside the window,
in the southern olive, beaten metal leaves
of Chinese chimes rustle, banging lightly.

We read the signatures of things, their signs,
of aspens, faces, free-falling sunlight
and the light that shines from stars.

Paris 1973

Every summer the Rio Grande takes
a lazy or ignorant or cocky kid
like a cold beer
and gives it back at its leisure
on or near July 4th.

This year it is Darren Vigil
who went in with jeans and boots.
The village searched the river
for two days to have his body
back for Mass.

Last year fever took Georgia age 11
and Yvonne Mascarenas
was flung from the Himalaya ride.

God forgives them.

It is always a river in one form or another.
We mourn them
as Saturday night flows by
filled with children.

The tiny cretinous heads blackening the ground
(a few neurons strung together by fibers)
are all females.
In the spring I watch them emerge —
little black ones climbing in columns
up the olive tree.
In the summer the males are born
— they look like wasps —
and swarm, take flight
followed by their larger slower queen.
They mate with her midair
and falling, dying, are dead
before they hit the ground
to be the meal of spiders, lizards
and other ants.

Sun beats down on snow at 12,000 feet
and the water runs through the gorge
to the valley below
and gets diverted by law and custom
into the fields of winter wheat and apples
where it dies for life.

The first settlers didn't mean for the acequias to last,
they just wanted to water their fields
in June 1815 so they wouldn't starve in November,
but they did last, running
on the north and south side of the valley
and are here today, 160 years later,
filled with water springing off the peaks
and dashing down the mountain
into the valleys, running into laterals
to the corn, squash, beans
and kitchen gardens with herbs.

Strange modest monuments
that make their way through the valley
and fall back, with what is left in them,
exhausted, into the river.

To the west, a village
of low houses and trailers
dusty in the winter light.
Can I say "my village"?
I haven't planted its fields,
haven't spilled my blood for it,
haven't made it mine.

There is much we don't have here:
soft rain, ambition, the sea.
We have deep cold and poverty
and the little river
that tumbles rocks in the spring
and becomes a trickle in the fall
and runs black under the ice in January.
We have a soil of clay and sand
that barely supports pastures and kitchen gardens.

We have rocks cactus dust
ants and an abundance of light,
horses cattle sheep dogs cats,
mice rats spiders bears skunks deer elk,
an occasional cougar,
doves and ravens and jays and magpies
and many different winds,
those from the south that bring dust,
others from the freezing north,
and from the east, from the mountains
where there is gold, a wind of minerals.

The first farmers had ancestral glimpses
of Extremadura and the voyage over
and no going back,
memories of caravans
from Chihuahua to this northern outpost
where they were abandoned
and buried alive under the blue sky.

There are a few farmers left
rooted in the present of excitable dogs
and placid horses,
cries of despair and defiance
rising into the cold blue sky.

A hot windy day with white clouds sweeping overhead
and the earth dry and rocky underfoot,
I wandered up a hill and stumbled on a camposanto
with brightly-colored plastic flowers faded to white
and wooden crosses tilting to the right and left and fallen.

At 7,000 feet, it was like standing on a tower,
while on the earth lay
abandoned crosses made of old lumber and homemade nails
and headstones that were large boulders or slabs of cheap cement.

I was pleased to be reminded of decay and death
but I didn't feel the awe I felt the first time
I walked through a camposanto in Ranchos, as a boy,
and felt the thrill of how dead the dead are.

Although the dust and neglect of the graveyard
are not to be treated lightly,
I don't see much difference
between the rainless clouds racing overhead
and the headstones with their laconic names and dates.

Arroyo Hondo 1976

Once he went to war
and stayed two years and had a mistress.
I learned this in my mother's milk
or looking back. The emptiness
which I can bear I do not want
you to have to bear. It is not
that I grew and left you
or you growing are leaving me.
My father did not abandon me.
Yet the anguish of lack is there
in him in me in you,
each of us orphaned at an early age.

What is this cry men cry
for their fathers
when they have one solid
and flourishing?
What is this search
for bone and hair?
Looking into the photo of you
in your army coat and hat,
finding nothing speaking,
a face that smirks
and does not speak to me
or fill my fathering emptiness –
my father, me, my son end
howling after a linked chain.

I handle you at my heart.
You are secure in my arms
until the day I break your trust.
I will not. I am here
large and dying for your warmth.

for Alexander

Downtown El Paso

"This white shirt
dark pants
and sturdy shoes
and the way I hit the book
softly and my manner
make you think
I'm crazy
but this is English.
Even unto to you bag lady
even unto you old man
I say all the stage
is giving way,
all the stasis
that surrounds us
is eroding.
I try to be succinct
I want to be
but no one listens
pimp-heads
punks
geezers
go ahead
fall asleep
at least I cry.

I admire the patience
of the pigeons
walking on your pock-
marked shoes

I admire
your tattoos
I'm not your usual ranter
I am not the subject
of this
          hiss
oh woolworths
oh jewels by barker
oh hotel du pre.
This could go on all night
so pass the bread crumbs

o farter
scum
and moldy toast
you won't be here
by morning,
none of this exists
wake up greaseball – oh
that got to you, nigger, spic,
Lenny used to do this turn
Lord, now it doesn't even harm.
All I ask is
react young tits,
your greaser has it up.
Listen short pants
we are all sinners
that is true
truer than I know
I won't forgive you.
I am capable of anger
sweet Christ spit on it
sweet lord, knock it down for me

and I am yours
knock it to its knees.
Every man his
own religion
This is good stuff
unrecorded
This is English
this is thirst."

The historian of zero

He studied Luther and wrote of Tetzel
and John Maier of Eck
and wrote well.
He researched three years,
wrote in eighteen months,
six more saw it into print.
The department prize in May
and one week later
first in the state fair fly-casting.
Married colleagues envied him
his leisure, his even temper
and his interests.

It is strange, he wanted more of life.

He wrote: "The use of zero per se
is not an obvious thought
like the ladle. The Arabs
in their glory revealed it."
He found the material
amounted to little,
practically nothing.
In the evening brandy
Wittgenstein and Mozart,
cast on Sundays
and wanted to cry
or hurt somebody
after European History one 0 one.

At his barbers
he desired the manicurist.
He wanted joy
and searched True Detective for it.
He grew gray, thinner,
a banshee lover,
and wrote his secret
history of the cipher.
They found him in a tenement
on his knees, depraved.
The papers would not give specifics.
He harbored his defense
and said the proofs
intrigued him:
$A + 0 = A$
$A \times 0 = 0$

His father was a doctor,
his mother half Jewish,
and he a social climber,
scribbler, pederast
without ambition or career
who had one mention
in the Almanach de Gotha
(that contained an error)
and dipped his Madeleine into tea.

Marcel, if you had to choose
living or remembering
which would you choose?

      It's a silly question.

Yes of course, but which?
Which makes you feel most alive?

      Don't make me choose. I cannot choose.
      One does not exist without the other.

I know but which? Most alive?

      Neither. Both.
      Besides it's death
      that makes me feel
      most alive.

The photo of the three of them
tells it all – too much –
the way he trails his wife
who was the first and only psychoanalyst in Sicily,
– a fat old man with a cane
and pants hitched up to the end of his tie.

And Gio – his adopted son –
slender and ironic
hand on hip
unaware that his "father"
contains a Leopard.

Great Jew!
Great American!
Neither.
Just Bobby Z
a simple genius with baffled hair
and no self
who wounded by Hibbing
wounded us,
who seeking himself
found us and flowed into us.

I know you Dylan, of my youth,
rebel attracted to crowds
and I in line with you
finding in your jumbled words
the torment of the wanderer
and the dying of identity.

What are you doing, moon
there in the sky?
Distributing madness?

I am haunted by other's lives
but I do not envy you
white, without words,
mirror of our distant lord.

Rhetoric

Being something of a voyeur myself
I loved your poem, its rhymes and alliteration
and the blue-shadowed silk
worn by Susanna in the green water
– but I was young, younger than she was.
Now I wonder at the rhetoric and the range
of devices that ornament the poem.
Why not just say the old men looked and loved?

I too like alliteration and can string it
line to line like Christmas lights
but *make music, so the self-same sounds*
is excess, to my mind,
and *pulse pizzicata of Hosanna* – really?

I respond to assonance too,
she stood in the cool of spent emotions,
those oo-s cooing like doves
but you have gone too far
with *simpering Byzantines and tambourines.*

Don't get me wrong; I get it;
if music is feeling then poetry is feeling too,
a verbal music that attempts to tie
our senses to ideas, an image to a thought,
using all the tricks at our disposal
such as rhyme, that antique ruse,
but you overdo it with
quavering and wavering

and when you seek to vary
and make them off, you go too far,
plays and praise, flame and shame;
masculine or feminine, internal or otherwise,
rhymes lose their luster in the end

for sounds ignite one portion of the brain,
while meaning – more sister than lover – another;
sound can sap the line of meaning
and leave us spell bound
and lead us to say things that sound like truth,
the body lies; the body's beauty lives
but aren't.

They say: root it in the sensual
and I, young sensualist, are more than willing
but eschew the abstract? Never.
For more than stars and planets,
the universe consists of empty space,
an abstraction if there ever was one.

Mother of my poems,
father of my thoughts,
my first love and with luck, my last,
images come easy,
stone, water, light –
Alas, sight is not vision.

Metaphor, that bedrock of poetry,
serves the purpose of joining this and that,
but *death's ironic scrapings*
and *the viol of her memory*
are not exactly brilliant or exact.

while its squire, simile, limps along,
its *refrain like a willow swept by rain*

and irony, that cat's paw,
last refuge of the lazy,
fortress of the skeptical,
dishing up small portions of significance
like over-cooked and over-spiced
blini au saumon fume

for irony annoys me, my own and yours,
when it lets the horrors of the world
off the hook and self-satisfied
moves on to look at something else.

As ceremony hides the heart's emotion
so rhetoric conceals four verities of life
– birth, love, labor, death –
which is why I say in un-ironic terms
that truth is served by clarity
and simplicity is best.
Who am I kidding?
All poems are made of rhetoric
trying to rise above rhetoric and failing,
striving to express what is eternal in the mind
but dying in the throes of fashion

and so, while I resist it,
poorer, I miss it,
and return to it as to a woman
who betrayed but loved me,
and vice versa, and all forgiven,
marry.

A poet wrote
we must love one another or die,
and later revised this to
we must love one another and die
and in his final years
he came to loathe the poem
and removed it from his oeuvre.

Yet life goes on, linear as ever,
and if we gaze at a truly ageless poem
    beauty is truth, truth beauty — that is all
    Ye know on earth, and all ye need to know —
we wonder had he lived, would he change it to
    truth beauty? beauty truth?
and later remove it altogether

for youth knows what youth knows, which is little,
age knows best, which is less.

Cavafy is as real to me
as living people.
My mother Kay
inoculated me
with literature,
rare instance
of catching the disease.

It meanders from brain
to joints,
arthritis of
generational words.

I drink too
and at forty
I look backwards and forwards
to more words, more drink.

It is afternoon
the sidewalk steams with rain.
I have heard that high fever
auctions off the future
consumes her singing.

A river in her arms
soaking the bed,
a little furnace in her
manufacturing fever.

Stop!
Hair sticking to her forehead
seaweed on the shore.
You, air-carried virus
going about town
seducing girls.

Am I jealous?
Do I mock the first suitor
or is there actually in her
a card shark
riffling his deck?

for Sara Kay

I saw a silver loop hanging from her ear
and glimpsed her loved by men and loving them.
This is love, to want her gone and living.
Then she moved. I saw the loop
was light caught in a curl.

      It waits
      suspended
water
      flowing from a spout
for me or you
      or my son to see
how it hangs
      suspended
not broken into component parts
           but continuously single

Sing this

To sit slightly
drunk abed
with you
and drink
a bit and still
do nothing
in the afternoon

not yet moved
except by the thought
of what awaits

or moved, yet
doing nothing
for a while

and then, do
what we love to do.

for Phaedra

In the dazed air through which I go
I kiss her everywhere occurs to me,
her lip, cheek and I kiss her hair.
It comes to me to kiss her neck,
her eyebrow and her nose.
In these silent days
this is music I create
for her to hear
when I kiss her everywhere.

Go friend into your cups alone.
You will not find me there.
I am forty-five and fading
                and literature, that activity
                of malcontents and wives
                who have the time
                and actors, clerics, landed poor
                        everyone in fact
                        taking a crack at it
                        like marriage and VD
                                dreaming of titles in a row
                                or achieving a line
                                an honest phrase
                                a bon mot . . .

Bulky,
interiorly sleek
admit to nearly continuously
devious thoughts
and dirty feet
Stripped of early
ambition
turning forty-six and fat

I
write
in secret

in defeat
am amplified.

Dec. 31
Indecorous day,
    my theme
        the fury
            of a certain age

and poetry
        drink-bidden
            there in the hand
embarrassing
    wry
        and used up

An ode to something
        sonnet
            or sestet
                something formal and green

an orderly going
        with my wits about me

but no,
    no art from
        the tag end
            of the year

None of the green
            onion,
not as long as art
        is linked
        to anarchy
and to the heart that doesn't know –

An orchard in bloom
    and warm gusts of air –
I would hang
      to have them back.

Instead
      the sobbing
of the old
      as it goes.

Todros, you give yourself to every barmaid,
Jewess, daughter of Arabia,
your eye is a great traveler,
your vision penetrates as deep as a well-thrown spear.
When the carnival from the south is in town
you find black beauties irresistible,
but the mule trains from the north
bring rustic miners' daughters.
Their eyes, you find them marvelous as long as they are green
or black or brown, and bright,
their lips full and curled, not in sneer – in jest –
or narrow, good for kissing;
their throats: long is good, short is fine,
their touch tender or rough or better, both.

Pull them all close, let the wind blow,
and afterward sing their praises
from the tops of Toledo's towers.

Wasp's nest

For days it sat there
it had not earned a place yet
it was moved from counter
to the window sill.
My wife brought it home
a curiosity.

Did it throb?

One kid is expected home at three
the other at three-fifteen
each afternoon the same
the daylight sinister.
I think I should have washed my hair.

alas old nest, emptied of your tenants

so I visit you as I would an empty house,
round, gray, fragile.

I listen at you, smell you

Be alive ruin,
be brave you brought-home ruin.

When I sank my roots into this town
I did not foresee the depths of my loathing.

The arithmetic of it escaped me:
cold nights, mud houses, arid orchards,
skies of grotesque clarity.

In Floyd's café on the last night of fiestas
we ordered coffee and posole
and watched the drunks fight.

Goodbye to a town that is dirt
and paradise to me, the rustle of horses
in the alley after the baseball game,
the walk through the park
congested with drunks.
We saw each other in a rotten light.
We said rude things.

What have you become? An unsubtle
travesty of dream-long centuries has resulted
in an old town becoming young again.
You pinch your pimples, comb your locks,
your hair is black, your shirt a flame.
I see you in cinematic terms
ropes around your boots
dragged through the dust of history.

Would I reach down into the under-
current of the place you are
and draw into the light

the rhythm of your loves
antagonisms and deceits?

Your hedges shine, your rough
waters curl, your rural slums
of cardboard roads
slouch past. It is the poverty

of your existence that afflicts me,
the mythology of a path capturing
the snow, the lyricism of three
strands of wire in April.

How glib love is, and spoken of, is worse.
The poets lie, the ancients lied:
they are grim, the roads to a town
where one's heart is.

*The rage among the tourists is to see Rosaria Lombardo
whom the master embalmed in arsenic.*

Nota 1918
Morta 1920

Your father kissed your eyebrows
and turned you over to Professor Salafia.
A half century later
the priests still cannot duplicate his work.

You were placed to the right of the corridor of clerics
in the western tier.
Sixty-five years dead and you look as human
as you did in life.
The bow in your curly hair
is as fresh as a violet.
American and German children come to see you.
You lie there in your open coffin,
perplexed.

Palermo 1985

In Syracusa we saw eleven Chinese
riding a bicycle of twigs that collapsed into a box.
It was a provincial circus where they threw swords into the air
and caught them in their teeth
and tumblers who prompted us to clap and sing.

Later we realized circus smiles cover a lot of sorrows.
So do the falls the clowns take
backwards into each other's arms.

On the ridiculous first day of spring
I walk around town
that is bright with rain and wind.
Seated in a nameless piazza
three Catholic girls suspicious
of me, gossiping in dialect
but I understand every word
of their cheeks and collars
and every hair.

And Bruno, hooded over the fruit stalls,
who cares if worlds are infinite?
G. Bruno burned here,
died in flames for imagination.
Not much selling
– lemons, fish.

I took my children to a cemetery
and walked through the stones –
a hundred, a thousand stones.

I dragged them through the slums
to see the needles in the gutters
and acres of wash.
Behold the dribbling idiot
who rushes up to us.

On Murano
we sat watching
apprentices sprouting
orange hot dolphins.

It was cold and a comfort
to sit in the heat of the workshop
watching the waves out the door.

Four of us, a family, alive
to the bonds that grow
over long meals of pasta and wine
in a foreign country.

Here in North Carolina we are horrified
at the profusion of large spiders
and how blatantly they attach their threads
to our windows and proceed to weave
large webs right there, in the glare
of our bedroom lights.

My wife is disturbed by them but photographs them
and adds their photos and descriptions of them
and their webs to the nature book
our children started, then abandoned
after school began.

One day while they were in school
she and I threw it all aside
and went to bed in mid-day like newlyweds.
We lay on top the covers in the humid heat
and made love as we had not in a long time.

Then afterwards instead of a cigarette
I got up to put on music
and there, very large,
in the center of her web,
a spider on the window staring at us.

And when, in a flash of spite,
I tapped the glass pane hard,
the spider did something violent in return,
struck at me, in defense perhaps,
or with pure aggression,
thinking to feed.

In 2006, Phaedra was poking around in the old Leading Edge computer and found a letter in the form of a poem I had written, the first one I typed on a computer, in 1986.

Dear Phaedra, Zander and Sara,

This is a new moment, writing on a computer,
a new genre, a letter with broken lines
speaking to you from solitude.
Word processing gives me the illusion of speaking with you in real time.
This is me, and I know that you are there, yourselves, in real time too.

I have been reading Henry Adams,
I am always reading someone.

They are like old friends very old in fact dead.
Leopardi the poet who wandered around his hometown
writing about how happy he was as a child
and Cavafy who believed that odd moments of sensuality
constitute eternity.
I agree with him: fragments of existence
are more real than speeches.
Thus I believe too that the moment
when I felt the wings of the present brush me
on a path in Rocca di Papa in 1960
altered life for me. I dedicated my life to those moments
and to seeking them in search of a salvation
that admits to none.

And now I am lost in a world
where words feelings and ideas merge
in a plastic box, silent and animated.
It is not me seated at a keyboard
but it is becoming me.
Music moves forward having nowhere else to go.
Poetry examines life with an x-ray
that sees with clarity the surface of things.

I am reluctant to impose my metaphysics onto you
but here goes.
Time flows on
and music and sunlight and love
are indestructible in their mutations.
All changes and yet does not and yet does.

Our assertions are our negations.
Let us embrace them.

Which?
I am lost in this thing
and realize ironic wisdom is a way to say
yes against the odds,
is my way of saying
us four, forever.

This typing is like a high wire act
with lots of nets
thank god for cut and paste, for save and delete.

I look out the window
and see how light is striking the trees
and I think how long it takes to love a landscape,
as long as to love a person and as mysterious.
What is most elusive is most real.

How convey the shore I sit on
observing the sea I see?
How say I know your shores, your seas,
how distinguish them from mine?
We are afloat
and time is busy
not as evil as it appears
nor as trust worthy.

I reach backwards to the people who sang about this
and know they had me in mind
and forward to you, who recognize me,
eager to talk and speak and love
and eventually to hold each other in the rising tide.

Cold sober, shaken, in a gleaming suit
and pale tie, I walk down the middle
of the tracks outside of Charlotte.

A pick-up with a rough engine
stops at a crossing
when the train approaches.

"I came to life at the crossing
I shine through the poor night.
Startled out of the station
I gain my stride between
High Point and Charlotte
dreaming, glinting . . ."

Today the young admire
those who spend the most.
Today there is no significant form.
I should know,
continental drift is nothing
compared to me.
Self-censored, void, a gridlock of impulses
in the cool morning.

Later, walking by the river
I see tracks
of birds in the mud.

To you, life-in-death,
I address this poem
that was never written.

I address you as you appear
in the form of a stone, a cross,
while you seek me
in the tracks in the mud
in the shadows in the pines, shy;
on the road that leads to the past.

First the harsh sounds
of mortars POUM POUM
and rifles CNT CNT
no one could keep them straight even then,
names like Buenaventura Durruti
and the spring time of Azana.

It was the prelude to the wholesale butchery
of the world's industrial-league war
and was itself pictured in 1819
by Goya's two Aragonese with clubs,
a human fight without elegance
but sunny – cold and sunny.

Fascist general Jose Millan Astray
who lost an eye, then an arm
said it plain as day –
Death to the Intellectuals
Death to Life.

We learned how sinister a leftist cell
can be flaying the leader
of the anarchist-syndicalists of his skin.

A conflict attended by invited
and uninvited guests,
catered by rivals.

A romantic war
when men fought in shirtsleeves
and were shot propped against orchard walls,
the bully nations

slipping in blows to the head
with 2 x 4s and axe handles.

So much for that war.
It made no sense
except the sense of right and wrong.
We knew then and proved again
by sheer inaction
which side we back
which side we are.

Then the final quiet sounds
of old posters
ripped in two
and disposed of.

"Aug. 12, 1707
John L. of Bath Towne
in the province of North Carolina
being of perfect mind and memory
calling to mind the mortality of my body
and knowing that it is appointed for men
principally and first of all
I give and recommend my body to ye Earth
and my Soul to Almighty God that gave it;
to my dearly beloved Hanna Smith . . ."

Lawson walked 1000 miles
through these woods
before there were white men.

A young Englishman,
in his innocence
the savages did not touch him
but guided him from tribe to tribe.

The wind blew gray moths
through mixed pine, oak . . .

Wanderer, writer,
surveyor of New Bern and Bath
and author of a history
of a place without one,
a forest where a Scot
was boiled for three days,
a searcher-out of lands
where savages were

numerous as spiders.
His book has the youth
of specificity still;
he thinks each apple matters
and its name and use.
He says good, well, pleasant, excellent
even though the Juniting is early ripe,
soon gone in these warm countries.

Lawson, hang your pages to dry
in the cabin in the woods-infested land,
for beyond the man who writes
his lists down
lies an added dementia –
the half-real who extracts
out of every time
a slice of not-real
and transmits it to the page
sister to life
ghost of a moth.

When he returned
they ran him through the forest
for two days,
inserted sticks into his flesh
and lit them
and he became a lantern of alarm
warning of insufficient embrace
of the Carolina woods.

Did he address them
as his agents of demise?
Did he continue to deny
the nature of the continent?
There is no date sung by

blind singers in taverns.
As his fate drew to
its exhausting close
was its obscurity a matter of regret?
At the moment when his death
was clear, did his life go before him,
a path through the pines
to a track of sunlight on the sea?

Goya speaking:

Meditation on life, that is on death. Positioning myself in the moment, I am trying to understand why one wants to live. Initially it is a given, as for a hunting dog or an oak, but after one has died, it becomes a question that something or someone asks. And on some level one should answer.

But I don't want to.

Although I painted these fourteen works fourteen years after my illness, they arose within me during the times of high fever and delirium.

I staggered out of the illness like a man out of the sea.

Here, this is how it was: thinking myself dead, I told the truth. I had nothing to lose or to gain. This one represents . . . that one represents . . . and once when I could celebrate the smooth red cheeks of a young woman, now her face is all mouth.

I died and voices died with me, song and music died with me. I paint shrieks I cannot hear.

Knowing I had to regroup I got to work but every topic, even the ones I had addressed before, were overwhelmed by ogres and freaks who sought me out and inhabited me. I had to paint them outside myself and here they are, product of the illness.

As for Leocadia, what a sweetie she is, with her laugh and her eyebrows, but in the face of fever, she withdrew. Who can blame her? Her thoughts grew practical. She came to wonder who would get the house and orchard. Peasant-like, I deeded them to Mariano, son of my son, warmth of my mornings.

Come to the end I expected to meet my mother. It made me smile, amused that I had reverted to superstition. The thought of her "waiting for me" was doubly funny pictorially and intellectually.

As with everything, I was impatient.

La Quinta del Sordo

"Guided by a friend, I returned in '26
to the house where I had lived and worked"

Walls dark
as if a fire
had raged
within the house.
A shock to realize
not soot
but paint.
The deaf man
went from work to work
and did not look
so much as touch
the paintings
with his eyes.

"Leocadia Weiss
welcomes you
a woman
beautiful, bored,
her skin and splashing eyes
once roused in me
the passion I felt for Rita Luna, the actress
who excelled in dagger roles
and mirror of my heat.
La Leocadia oversaw the washing
meals and me

but in my illness
she recoiled.
She leans upon our bed,
high tomb of all my hopes.

Any old man can tell you
that the old are ravenously
envious of the young, that getting old is a sin
without redemption.
The horror of a human
eating a human
surpasses understanding.

The man who eats his own
is despicable of course
but try to appreciate
his own terror.

I painted this feast
where once I heard the sounds of the procession,
jumbled snatches of carriages
distant corks and laughter.
Dreaming of youth
is a senility similar
to a dog running in its sleep.
Now the right and religious
lead the way,
grandees and their nuns
sullen with desire.
I have come to understand the vices
and portrayed them here as a procession
of men and women bloated by hypocrisy,
the fearful faces of the godless
pressed against the superstitious pious.

Here, no man knows the hour
of his death
but I have depicted
an old man
deaf as lead-white
with his wall-eyed friend
whispering in his ear
the date place time
and circumstances –
call it the whisper.
Now can the voice inside
differ from the friend's ?
Is it Hallelujah, hallelujah,
or Time to go?
Doesn't matter.
He can't hear.

The fight is a peasant's affair
Aragonese and as eternal
as the sands.
Implicit in the scene
are their long hard births,
minimal education, this moment,
ending with mourners, singers . . .
The eloquence resides
in the clockwork of the blows
and in the cattle scattered in the sunlight.

The Holy Office, stop and think
how appropriate the name.
I like to match
those who torment
with those they torment,
the executioners

and the puppets.
And the dog. Not to make a deal of it,
the dog is loyal, apprehensive,
and fawns upon a being in the distance,
his master whom he cannot see.
The dog is real if paint
and has more dignity
than creatures of imagination.
I sentimentalized it
as I could not greed
and lust and gluttony.

No longer capable
of studding pictures
with topical references,
I painted these without the patience
or ambition of May second or third.
I could have named the series
sins and sleep.
They are what appeared to me
in illness, as faithful
as I could recall.
I see them lifted off the walls in fifty years
and carted to the capital
entombed in a well-lit place.
In a hundred years
the suppressed and privileged
will butcher Spain again
the faces of the godless
up against the church-shocked citizens,
the clicking sound
of untracked history
drowning them
in ease and emptiness.

No not said right
a singer can sing
a momentum towards darkness
which, if proclaimed, proclaims
his innocence and ignorance.
This is how it was.
I painted images to hold in check
the pain and the oblivion
of living, images to drown
demented thoughts
about unreasoned acts.

I hid these away
to hide the pleasure
killing gives me,
I am rested when
the world is revealed
as sinister and loathsome.
It is hard to explain
and has to be said
with irony, irony
mixed with inevitability.
These rooms were dark
and I painted with candles in my hat,
deaf as a stick I painted as if blind."

I have found minor gods, nymphs and satyrs,
in sunlight and rivers,
in the flesh of women and the faces of children,
in sports and the underworld of chess and Go,
in wine and LSD
and in the cawks of ravens and the hooting of doves,
in ink – mine and others

but my true love, a great god, is Death,
not the many small deaths we experience in life
that are more comical than tragical,
but the abstraction that rules all my thoughts.
The body dies but the soul!
The soul dies too,
and I welcome Death as a release
from a life of anticipation and disappointment.
Death is more powerful than life.
That is what I have been trying to say for some time.

Banged-up one, who lunged face
first from your stroller
into the pavement of Poros,
allow me to suggest
that this is not the end
of your spills.

You cannot anticipate the next plunge
or imagine the metaphysical ones at all,
but a moment waits when you glimpse them
and the forces of buoyancy
that carry us from fall to fall.

for Alexandria

You climb into the voices of the young,
you erode the horse's stride

yet you bring into my life
a solace, rust on iron
decay of wind across the mud flat

I address you, death,
against a morning somewhere
when one of us is going down
and deeper.

Still I wonder why
the sky is so blue
and the water so green.

The poor of the
eastern provinces
want a voice.
We all want voices
shrill low sad
but doing something with them
is another matter.
The rest is silence.

Some want stories,
knots and footprints,
eyes to see:
what wild longing
to cry and see.

And others to get buried
with the king
and embrace the final cup.

I cannot judge.
I vacillate between
the blue vein of blood returning
and the bleeding red.

I remember the way
light lit the sill,
firelight falling
on the red floor,
the blue and the wind
that preceded the rain.

I remember
your black hair,
the color of your skin
and your lips,
the mud
and running water,
the silhouette
of the mountain range
and the fields we lay in.

Simply in those nights
we created glory
that resembled truth.
We loved and fell on each other
without thought of the morning.
When I took you you sank
into the field like water gone forever.
I took you
because you had no name
no past

and I was taken
by a womb
ripe with Alexander.

I would like to be precise here
in the Latin manner,
about two souls walking in the park.

I want to say this with some restraint,
with words that do not hurt or frighten you,
about what time is doing to our love.

I want to but cannot,
the very pain that causes me to speak
prevents me and silences my heart.

I drew two babies
into my embrace,
then threw them
into air,
high into space
in the knowledge
I was there to catch them.

This they knew
in the wisdom
of being infants.

Now I throw them
into the world
and they know
I am not here.
I have gone
to another place.
In the fullness of love
I leave them suspended.

Enough. It is over.
You exist. I had my run
at ecstasy
and leave the stage
to you.

"I am breathless
egotistical one. Leave me
room for my myths.
I am dubious and wet,
an irony I cannot ignore or forget.
I breathe air daily,
I swim as strongly as you
and know corners
you do not. I see lights
that blind you.
My trains wail. Leave
them passage through."

It's taken me half a lifetime
to understand what Dante wrote.
I thought it was foolish of him
to idealize a young girl
he scarcely knew
based on the curve of her cheek.

Now I am inclined to love
a woman I saw today
on the basis of her curls,
the same curls that loomed
over me before.

I am not free Your smooth
cheek has captured me You
infect me with your long legs
You have entered me You
and your long lashes
your angular jaw and Your
earnest assessment of love.

I bury myself in you
and lick you I Wonder
if you like it
as I like it I sense
that I have fallen
for an image of myself Dark
sardonic wise-cracking woman.

Young woman
with eyebrows
I look at you
you look at me
but I see you
and I see the end
of every gesture
in your eyes
you cannot guess
how soon I see the moment.

In each house
the black gap
of a fireplace
You know
don't you
the source
of illicit love?
If I could capture
the knowledge of
impending guilt
this leap . . .
this loss . . .
and how subtly the past
consumes the present.

I see you and you are not
who I see.
This is a moment
worth pursuing to its end
in irony and song.

I see you
I do see the air.

Let's set some ground rules:
we don't tell our friends
or write this up in our journals.
We stay stoned throughout.
We agree on the music
and try at least two positions.
We won't wear each other's clothes
or in the morning call it love.
We'll call it what it is

List of things to bring:
your pride, intact
and tactile humor
and your eyes
they are mine too,
your appetites
and your flaws
which I brush with my lips.

I will bring a knife for fruit
and to slip into your heart,
a small bottle
for mouthwash or tequila.

Open your mouth
open your legs
open your eyes;
these are crude
and fleeting days.

We will get drunk
so I'll bring pesos to bribe you
to do something you are reluctant to do.

What are you packing that
you don't want me to see?

We will need our wits about us.

While I sat on the beach
facing Antarctica and darkness,
you waded in the ocean's edge

Later I saw on the thin blanket covering you
stems, flowers, leaves

It is so odd, two strangers
who stick themselves into each other
for pleasure

In an hour you will be forty-five,
a forty-five year old woman

You winced when I said that
so I said it again
and grew hard saying it
and entered you again,
odder still, and older.

On the walk home
I saw the emblems of our lust:
two naked dolls, bald and eyeless
placed cheek to cheek in a sand box,
a bored dog gnawing on a stick,
a house neglected by the landlord,
its paint peeling and porch sagging
in the winter sunlight.
It is not that I am bored
although I am very bored
or that I am tired
although I am exhausted.
It is not that I am wiser:
I have learned more jammed
up against her than from all the books;
it is not that passion has diminished
along with muscle tone
or that I can't see stars.
It is
my experience is
love is never met with love,
love transmutes with time
and grows vicious with time.

And after his son flew
into the sun and fell,
he continued over the sea
riding his gigantic wings

or,
heartbroken,
he skimmed the waves
            then sank
            quickly
            his tools clamped to his back.

"The ebbing class"
               Codrescu

I feel less and less
I tell them this,
they don't believe me

It is a strange sensation,
the death of my heart

The trick of costume dramas
is to drop the costumes
as the play unfolds

In the mirror, a lopsided
face I have fled,
an eye that cannot see itself.

She comes out of the shower
with a cap of wet hair like a boy.

She simply wants me to want her;
it is what most girls want.

Two in the afternoon
we sit in the backyard
listening to the drone of a plane.

The air is howling with a fire siren
followed by a police siren
and then dogs imitating the sirens.

All this because of a 911 call?
At least someone is dying.

*When I resigned from the Boulder Housing Authority
I gave notice a year and a half in advance. Before I
left, I attended a two-day retreat for senior staff in the
mountains. We were asked to sing a song or read a poem
after dinner. I read the following.*

Two hours ago I was sucking on her.
She seemed to be enjoying it
but who knows?
Now I am sitting half-strangled by my tie
listening to voice-mail.

People return my calls.
A fat girl and a bus go by.
Everyone on our staff
claws for time to dream
and drink and go bowling.

This memo, to file,
could get me fired
or at least cast doubt
on my reliability

but it won't
because
I quit.

Crossing from El Paso
to Juarez at six in the morning,
Mexican soldiers ordered us off the bus
and made us line up
and open our bags.

A man had a box wired shut
too heavy to lift –
they clipped the wires
and tools spilled out.

Another man, a vaquero,
was made to drag his saddle off the bus.

A soldier slipped his hands into my bag
and under my clothes
and lifted them
as if weighing them.
I was afraid he would find
my lust and my fear.

Later, when the long Mexican bus
swayed down the highway
on sixteen wheels
I died escaping.
I thought of when my teeth chattered
with malaria like castanets.

These deaths
do not compare
to the one in you.

Before there was laser surgery
you lost an eye
age three

Your dad
bought you a glass eye
for your 7th birthday

Each year for fourteen years
he bought a new one

You played with the old ones
like marbles
and buried them in the backyard

I met you age 47 at a sidewalk café
in Morelia, your real eye
no longer as alive
as the round amazed glass one.

I saw you in three outfits:

On a motorcycle,
stocky in a linen skirt and man's shirt,
your bitter face animated with love
for the young man in a leather coat.

On the order of the madame
you dressed in a pink halter and pink shorts
and sat sullen with two vaqueros,
your thick lips painted pink.

The next day (it was a small town)
I passed you, a teenager
in jeans and denim jacket
defiantly walking alone to the market.

I died. My thick hair, irony
and hunger died.
News came in the usual way:
phone screams, a voice full of self
but I didn't expect this particular call.
I take refuge in practical details –
will they sink me in the ground
or cremate me?
The word spreads,
they send me to the hilltop cemetery,
it has snowed
but the sun is turning
snow to mud.

A variety of people come
fucking and eating on their minds.
Several could not get there in time
and one is way too busy.
Some spoke poetically of
"this dark flesh air-mailed to oblivion"
and "finished, the day, the bottle"
"Good looks" "half blind"
The simple coffin
by the slippery grave.
"He would have wanted it this way"

One articulated that poetry
is discovering the connections,
another said it is love
and read a poem, her own,
grass flowed and brandy.

My son reminded them
I preferred cremation.
Kerosene appeared
they lit me
they burned me coffin and all
one woman danced,
three thought to throw themselves
onto the bier.
My friend grieved,
my daughter looked across the valley
at my mother and the apple tree
a headstone of exuberance.

That night the fire in the stove
mirrored the sun descending,
and the heat of their faces
as they thought up epitaphs

    Here's our go-to guy
    yesterday a youth
    today, much less.

    No wife of his
    returned to men.
    Being suspect
    he suspected.

    Look, here lies a man
    equal gusts of love and death
    victim of a swipe across the eyes
    filled with floaters.

"**I** give until I'm faint
I give until the blood breaks
I give to belly
until the flood
You take
you break the bank."

There is no one who wants
to hear any of this
I run you through my mind
and find each of you
wanting more,
has your own life
and is bored by this,
even the oldest finds
his own life more interesting
and the youngest does not remember me
from visit to visit,
the ladies love me
as long as I love them,
my sisters are caught in the gears of illusion,
my friend is in love
and yet . . . this fabulous yet
only these ghosts matter,
they are my ghosts
and my love my lust for them
is alive in the bloodless art
I practice.

How did a timid woman
birth a fat and blubbery boy
who could not say
Ticonderoga's t,c,d,r,g?
The wind that blows against my skin
is the same that blew against you
fifty years ago,
this same light struck you then,
but why seek life in you, again?
I never asked what does it mean?
I never said do you remember, when, we . . .
Instead I said I am myself
but I was not.

You watched the sunsets,
sipped scotch and water
from a round glass
to dull the twilight,
retreated into sorrow
that I could not name,
did not acknowledge
until now.

Now I know it well,
it flows through me.
I sink into reverie
of your face.
I too watch dark gather
and time strike at sundown.
I no longer ponder why
I am arranged this way.

Cataracts blurred your sight,
you had them fixed
first one then the other,
I did not come to you.
My retinas fell off
first one then the other
and being dead,
you did not come to me.

But when you died I was there.
This sky, this light on water
remembers us together.

I loved you and released you,
I bestowed myself beside your bed.
Where your heart flowed
I flowed too.

Day turns to dust then night
so love, beyond love
to something else.

I did not know
that I was taken too.

No I never saw her as a hot number,
just a solemn young woman who wanted to feel desire.
She had long eyelashes and ripened breasts
and thought the world would end at 2000.
When her round eyes widened
and the pupils were exposed
I believed anything possible,
astral travel, end of the world, even love.

I won't go into details,
people think it crass.
Let's say it was seventeen days in October
and the way the yellow wind
rattled the silvery aspen leaves
provoked us to ecstasy.

Smitten, the first irony escaped me.
Doomsday me stood up for life
and she lay down damned
all afternoon and into the night.

We talked a lot too
and I hung on her words
and the way her lips formed them.
She felt like ivory and silk to me
and when she left
we vowed to meet again.

It's time to tell the truth
it's time – again –

not the truth about the world
which is vicious and trivial

not to tell my story
my story is one phase of the moon
not to tell your story
your story another phase of the moon

not the truth about the way
things were between us
dying separated by the torque
that twisted you one way
and me another

the truth about life
told without irony or pathos
the truth that is more mired in love than in hate

Is it too late to tell the truth?
I've slashed and burned many times
and the soil is still fallow

I wished you dead
I wished her dead
I wished everybody dead
but that is not the truth

The truth is
I am incapable of telling the truth
even if I could I wouldn't
even if I would I couldn't

Maybe truth resides in shame
about my mouth closing around this or that,
my penis penetrating this hole or that,
truth as outhouse serving a lower purpose
oh father let us sublimate

or should I simply tell the truth about
where we come from and where we go
. . . a speck in sunlight
        blown by the wind.

When I first loved them
they were children
soon grown breasts and hips
moving in a four-step hand to hand
gardenia-powered sweating perfume.
I aspired to sinning in the dark,
what they wanted was less clear.

Two small blue slippers
became a girl
composed of innocence – not a cell;
virtuous – below the waist,
lively breasts, lively tongue
and most of all, lively eyes
that teased the largest boy.
My dazed hands went
where my dick was not allowed.
Five years I bruised her neck
she my heart.
Whose fault is it
that I hid my lust
for that which she withheld?
I hurt and learned
how dry sex works.
Because I tapped the gong
and could not make it ring
I left her for a foreign shore
reverberating with regret.

I learned to proceed with another
from inadvertent touching
to holding, smiling looking
a drink a meal
then lip to lip under the streetlight
breast to chest under the porch light
and in the kitchen,
hand beneath the skirt,
further revealing of feelings.
I kissed her and she kissed me back
in a tidal movement toward the bedroom.

I was intrigued by her voice
her haunch her hair
her sofa songs bed songs
I felt the conqueror.

I of course mistook the evening
for a kind of happiness:
the seductive music, the dusk-like light,
the object of desire dissolving into me,
two raw paints ground together
to become a color mimicking the sky.

Why stare at me like that?
Because you are broad
where I am not,
because you are soft
when I am hard?
I open my bill to hiss at you
and you say I am singing.
You named names,

have I been charged?
I want to touch, not be touched.
Crippled three times, four
I shrink with horror from the weak ones
and cringe before the ones with power
which is all of you.

Goodbye to Persian rice
breast of chicken and cheap white wine,
silken hair, pale green sheets
fumbling off of clothes
slim smooth skin
mouthing on protuberances
words stopped by cock or cunt,
straight sex, doggystyle
69 and she on top,
ass fucking
synchronized or roped
horizontal vertical,
quick or yogic
soundless screaming.

Goodbye to slippery women
attached to hair, eyes, mouths
and all the rest,
a final fuck and I am gone
payback for heartbreak.

Voluptuous pleasure
of finding a room
in Andalusia
with a window
table, hard bed,
unpacking my clothes
and papers
then walking through the town
past the houses
following a path
out into the pasturelands
and wild grasses.

The tip of a waterwheel
rose like the sun revolving,
a waterwheel lifting water out of a river
and dumping it into a trough
that carried it to the fields.

That night, watching girls circle the plaza one way
and boys the other,
lights strung from trees,
music from one band brushing up
against the music from another,
I remember the wooden cups of the waterwheel
gripping the water and carrying it up.

Town workers dim then kill the lights,
the bands disband, the birds fall silent
and the wheel carries water up and up
until it falls into the trough
and flows into the field.

The river drives it
yet it lifts the river.

The hills here have the curves of a woman.
Sunlight clothes the peaks.
This is my landscape
of stones and trees.

Antonio Machado walked in these fields
not thinking, he was not a thinker
not feeling, his feelings died with his young wife.
What was he doing?
What I do.

It is afternoon,
a storm gathers.
Chalky light falls
on the cliffs in the distance.
Or is it snow? In March?

Light rain
I could see from the way
she plucked at the lint
on my pants
that the transaction
made her as sad
as it made me
but we had our masters,
hers downstairs and mine within.

Afterwards I got disoriented
in the Judaria.
I swore I was headed uphill
but ran into the river
at the Puente Naranja
and stood in a stupor
looking at the municipal waterwheel
lifting and dropping the river.

The bounce of the boards under my feet,
wood weathered by air heavy with salt,
a bucket of bait left unattended
and gulls ride the air –

past the benches
to the end of the pier
and listening to the water washing against the pilings
and looking at the line where the sea
merged with the sky.

I died there on the end of the pier
the emptiness inside
finally matching the emptiness outside.

I read, I can't remember where,
the first line of a book
"I walked out the door into the day and . . ."
he walked out the door at dawn
and walked all the way to Spain
and walked around Spain
meeting gypsies and barmaids.

Someone else wrote
and I can't remember who
"I walked a level road in the heart of a fruitful country."

. . . daybreak, on foot, it is all I have ever wanted,
leaving the city for the countryside
or better, leaving the country for another country,
on foot, at daybreak.

Because you're new, fresh, and what waits is romance
and acts of love and inspired poems
and you add them all together and get an adventure
whose first move is, I walked out the door . . .

which is well
but walking out and leaving familiar flesh
and the dogs and the bed
and the books and the blue of the front door
into the vacuum of the world
peopled by barking drunks
and skinny women in damp rooms
who suck you dry
is an adventure of a different kind,
the last move in a desperate game.

New place without furniture

First light at 5:45,
miraculous sight from my bed
of pale light behind the mountains
and a thin sliver of moon.
I make coffee in a frying pan
and sip it out of the pan.

8 a.m., sitting on the patio,
the sun clearing the plum tree,
a blast of light and warmth.

At 10, now is the time for me
to welcome the disorder of time
that stops and flows.
Now is the time
to create a factory for ecstasy,
intellectual ecstasy inspired by the stars
married to sensuous ecstasy rooted in the earth.

There is a photo
        of Anthony Martinez
                in this week's paper
a 27 year old
        seated at a bench
                making a bulto,
light from the window
        falling onto his hands

When he played center half
        in the youth soccer league
I saw him orchestrate two goals
        against my son's team

He became a hood
        smoked grass at school
                and was detained
for punching his girlfriend
        who had a daughter;
                later for burglary.

Far from home,
        in the penitentiary on the plain,
                he said he had changed his ways.

Now he is in the folk craft program
        that is funded by the probation department
learning to make santos and bultos
        like his grandfather.

Caught in the coils
of five centuries
they lived in the valley of Velarde
and came out at Christmas,
a family named Mondragon
deciding they are Jewish.

They rose as from the grave
red-haired and shocked,
they remember now, the rituals.

The village shrugged.
It always knew them
by their hair
and metaphysical sadness
which they hid and flaunted.

It changes nothing,
they still run their store
and plant in May.

When we find fossils of sea animals
embedded in stone on the high peaks
we admire how alive they were
in the shallow warm waters of northern New Mexico.

The pueblo, gangs, fiesta queens, bankers
will be under water again,
not in the shallow warm waters of northern New Mexico
but in the deep dark waters of the universal future.

1

Don't look directly at the sun, they said.
Its brightness will blind you.
I didn't listen and I looked.

Don't look too hard at women, they warned,
their hair will kill you.
Of course I looked – and loved.

2

The trick is simple, snaps into place:
take it as it comes,
devour when it's fat and suffer when it's thin,
embrace spring rain.

Padre Martinez writing to his cousin in Mexico

You know I came sincerely to spread
the Word of God the Father,
I came filled with celibacy and Spain
and four hundred lemon seeds on my tongue
and fourteen casks of wine

but here I am father, husband, priest
and now I love women, wine and Mary Corn and Joseph Rain
most of all I love the printing press and the weekly word.
I feel no shame,
it is a way of defying time to string out type
and record legalities and public news and remedies and plantings.

Up the hill on a dirt road, then off to the north
on a path through the piñon trees
toward where Babuk and Jan lived three winters in a teepee.
It is autumn before the first snow,
the trees hiding the dark mountains to the east
and the abstract plains to the west.
Babuk was a draft dodger who never uttered his real name,
a tall quiet man who played the flute as he walked out of the hills.
Jan, his wife, had a round blond placid face and blue eyes
and their baby with the same round face and wide blue eyes.

That was twenty years ago.
Alongside the path, white stones that I put in my pocket
for my mother's grave.

For Caroline S. Levy

I planted you at 7000 feet in an urn between two boulders.
You would have been eighty-seven today
a mean and desperate eighty-seven
with no girl left in you.

"This is my grave?"
"Mom it's beautiful."
"It is nonsense."
"What would you prefer, a headstone in Queens?"
"You should have thrown my ashes over the ocean."

I remember
        the cigarette you lit
                while one already burned
        the scotch and water
        and the way you scowled
                at the edge of the table
                        that interrupted your journey
                                from kitchen to bed.
In the morning
        the stench of black ash
                in the ashtrays,
        the stench of scotch
                watered to a thin piss
                        of failed oblivion.

Here in New Mexico it was different –
a book, a cigarette and a walk in the sunset,
your days passing like shadows on the ground,

a tranquility resembling despair.
We have that in common and trouble seeing
and difficulties in love and loyalties.

What a strange impulse
              to put you in a place
                          overlooking my house and family.
I come up here in the afternoon
              and watch the west
                          drink the light.

I could at least learn the names
              of the grasses
                          that poke up between the stones.
I pluck them out as if tidying you up.
They are winged, arid
and survive the winters year after year.

In a couple of years
I won't be able to climb this rocky slope.
It is time to cut a path across the hillside
and mark the way with cloth tied to piñon trees.

So much time has passed.
I don't know where you are.
Not under these white stones,
not hearing the sound of hammer blows from the village
or enjoying the dusk rising like water in the valley.

You were so right,
              so wrong
                          about everything
but to believe in anything
              is to betray you.

I could not deliver you from death
but I can honor your resting place
with words and silence.
I could not swipe the tears from your eyes
but I can speak to you of my suffering.
I finally see
how terrible how bitter
          how beautiful
your saying to me
          Go, live.

I did.

Let's face it
whizzing along on a twisting road
at 90 miles an hour
on my birthday
is not the height
of wisdom.
I could spin out
into the path
of a truck
or into the pines.

Instead I arrive shaken
and exhilarated.
Even before we speak
I look into your face
and the feeling is there
of recognition of how
much time has passed
and can we recover love,
struggling in the wake
of ecstatic nights
drowned in confusion.

for Phaedra

And only now am I
writing it down truthfully:
although I try to live in Spain, China
in books and ideas
        I live here
        I am me
        I am too much

too much flesh
too much mind
too much resentment
altogether too much
and when the roar is over
too much ash and bone left over

I would be air

I saw a procession of peasants coming down the mountain. I have seen them for many years and I recognize them – they are all identical, all joyous and indifferent – they have my number but it is not personal. They smile and – descending – they take my life. I used to think there was only one but there are many. They walk as if dancing and inside, they are emptier than any human can be.

I see them differently now. They are eternal and they took my mother and they took my friend and they will take me and then in time they will take my children. A different breed, they are smiling because they do not doubt.

they descend
with a light step
a shuffle
Are they dancing?

I have to smile
They are inviting me to shuffle too

It's that little shuffle
          within the dance
a barely detectable stumble
          – they've been drinking

a hesitation,
as if they are having second thoughts
or have forgotten something
something human
that leads to something

I now resist them. I learned in the sea that I have insights they do not. I have the desire to revolt. I smile and shuffle down the mountain as if I am one of them but — my secret — I decide to triumph.

I have seen this triumph in the faces of old people but did not know what I was seeing. I have touched it but it is like touching a bubble. It has touched me, when I am the bubble. I wish I could describe it better than this, for it is the resolution of dark and light and sorrow and joy. I experienced this vision in the strangest circumstance — in Fort Metal Cross in Ghana when I had malaria and in Ajijic (they came down from the hills). The inclination is to overcome my fate and I experienced it most powerfully in the sea off Oaxaca. In the depth of the darkest acceptance, there is hope, life, and love.

Then it is time to eat. Enough of the descending, as my mother would say, revealing her roots. I am tired of these peons coming down through the maize. Let them come through the outskirts into my world — a café with chairs on the sidewalk; let them come in through the front door (if the owner will let them) into the big room with mirrors and a long bar and tables — my table — where I eat olives and eggs and strips of beef and I drink wine and read and — here's the part I like best — write in my journal. What peasants they are in the face of my journal which, although not full of wisdom, is at least full of words.

New year's eve

There were delights:
your long legs and my ordering
another rum and Coke for us
and how good the real you sang along
with the jukebox

and the best part,
driving home shouting and pounding the wheel
and we got drunk and talked 'til two
and finally got down to what was on our minds
until we passed out
and in the morning we were
not really ready for the morning.

The lust part was the time
we spent in bed, I impersonally loving your long waist
and hair I pulled like reins
and when the ceiling spun
that was the last half hour of the year.

We were secret lovers
because I was your boss.
When I arrived on Saturday afternoon
I found you ironing a shirt to wear on Monday.
We washed away the work week
with two, three, sometimes four rum and cokes.
I entered you
and we mixed our joys and sorrows.

You with your long runner's legs and small breasts
and me with blurry eyes and uncombed hair,
you aligned to money and me to words.
How did we, both lovers of women,
come to love each other?

Sixteen years later
I remember being aroused by you
standing in a green bra and panties
ironing the shirt.

Glossy black hair
wide shoulders
but it is your long slim legs
I remember most
and the heat from the iron on a winter day
and the hiss of sprinkled water
and the taste in my mouth
of Coca-Cola and white Bacardi.

The mountains are green and granite before the first snow,
green and granite that flows from south to north
like a pod of whales, a pack of dogs,
electricity leaping from pole to pole.

They come close, encroaching on us
like dark thoughts. The next day they recede
green and tranquil as a calm sea.

In certain summer light
the mountains flow north
while the clouds rumble south
and me, by the road,
undecided which to catch.

I'd go north and find a room
and finally write something
from the heart that empties me
and I'd be finished

or I'd go south to where the women are
and drown in sunlight.

Instead I wait
fascinated by the flow.

A path between piñon trees
then down into a wide meadow
of chamisa, sage and wild grasses

Above, white sleeping mountains
Below, the earth is soaked with melted snow

The dog courses ahead
and goes into a stand of trees
but I stop, lift my head
and contemplate
being in the middle of a meadow
        alone, at peace,
                in a familiar dream.

Amplified voices from down by the river
testing the sound system

then chants accompanied by drums

Some are deeply mournful,
others upbeat

In between songs,
words in Tiwa,
dedications or a description
of what a song celebrates or decries.

The sounds of Tiwa songs
abolish the present,
resurrect the boy I was
roaming the town, the smell of popcorn,
lights of the softball field
and how intrigued I was watching,
among the Pueblo singers and drummers
in the town gazebo
a small boy in feathers and leggings
doing the hoop dance perfectly.

Thunder clouds rolling across the sky
gray in the center, white and silvery on the edges
like floats in a parade: The Great Boot,
and the Swan Seeking Leda

clouds coming over the mountain
like inevitable forces of history

and there, I see them clearly
a Hammerhead Shark
and a Dark Longboat
plunging through the surf

A storm is rising.
Clouds fill the sky, massive and threatening
and thunder is threatening

then the wind before the storm

I could go to the house now,
leave the apple tree, the horse, the weeds,

or wait and be soaked by the rain

More thunder,
thunder I heard in summertime in Taos,
the sky darkened and I was out
in the mesa on foot, eleven years old,
under the crack of thunder.
What did it mean, to mean, then?
The smell of dust in my nostrils,

a sleepy sexual feeling
coursing through me,
the air was electric.
Hispanic waitresses in the backdoor
of restaurants glancing up,
wondering, rain?
or only thunder?
as they watched the smoke from their cigarettes
rising into the clouds.

S.S. United States, New York to Calais, September 1960

In the morning several inches of snow
clinging to the branches of the olive tree
and covering the field below
but it is April and by noon
it has burned off the table and chair
and I sit outside with the two dogs
under the immerse blue sky
with a dual-language book of poetry:
Salvatore Quasimodo's selected poems

He said
> Io voglio partire, voglio lasciare quest'isola,
> I want to leave, I want to leave this island

and she replied
> O caro, e tardi: restiano
> O love, it's late: let's stay

and yes, I, listening, smiling,
each word touched my nineteen years.

He wrote
> Il tuo dono tremendo
> di parole, Signore,
> sconto assiduamente.

> For your tremendous gift
> of words, I pay
> assiduously, Lord.

and he wrote

> E qui nella notte, dolce agnello
> ha urlato con la testa di sangue

> And here within the night, mild lamb
> has howled with head of blood

which made me howl with pity,
terror and the beauty of the world

and he wrote

> Allora mi misi lentamente a contrare
> I forti reflessi d'acqua marina
> che l'aria mi portava sugli occhi

> Then slow I set myself to count
> the strong surges of sea water
> the air bore up into my eyes

and before me, for the first time
the sea revealed itself
as classical fire that consumes us.

After trooping over muddy roads with the dogs
feeling nothing except nothing
I sit outside listening to Shostakovich
wondering where the impulse to write poetry has gone.

The last spasm is to write
about not being able to write.

No one likes my incoherencies.
What I have to offer is silence
and degrees of death.
Degrees of death?
Is that my mission, to gauge them?

On a blue-bright day
I go into the house to get a hat
through the kitchen where the faucet gleams,
through the hall into the dark bedroom
where a sliver of light from the nearly closed curtains
shines in a strip across the wooden floor

and a memory of another bright day, age twenty,
in Florence, finding the iron door of a mausoleum
ajar and entering into the odorless space
and not understanding what it means to live if we die
or why anyone would put the dead in the dark
instead of outside, in the green, floral
festive garden the Italians call a cemetery.

Sitting outside with loose papers on my lap,
a gust blew the top two pages away.
It was a poem that contained some creatures
and the usual clouds and mists
and how fossils feel about mountains.
Like a Borges story, it contained the past and future
and how time distorts yet fuels our ability to love.

I jumped up and chased it down the road,
the poem containing metaphysical doubts
about existence, my own and yours,
and some truths too
and how everything doesn't mean anything
and it listed the questions that answer themselves
– am I capable of praise?

But it was gone, my best poem ever,
eaten by cactus or the wind.

If I could resurrect one writer to be with this afternoon
with this bottle of wine,
it wouldn't be Lowry,
he would drink the bottle in a flash and disappear,
or Lawrence, who would lecture me,
or Kerouac, a silly man.

Perhaps de Cunha, a solid engineer
or Martin du Gard, who has a capacity for friendship
or better, someone who is now obscure,
but not Pessoa, he is too shy
and there are too many of him.

Forget it. Call my dog. She is lying in the warmth
left in the grass, the creature who understands me best.

No Germans need apply
or Swiss or Scandinavians,
Russians are too emotional
Li Po talks too much
Plath is obsessing about Hughes
and Hughes is obsessing about some other woman,
Mudd is not dead yet.
None of the drunks – there are so many –
none of the academics for obvious reasons.

Stendhal is a possibility.
We could talk Napoleon, Italy and opera buffa,
or Marquez, but he just died and may still smell.
Lorca, Proust, I doubt they would find me attractive.

You know where this is going.
A sad and solitary man
who loved a teenage girl who died,
he taught, wrote a few poems,
loved a married woman,
fled Franco to France and died there
of a broken life.

I imagine a medium price white wine from Soria
and we talk but by the third glass,
he cuts the thread between us
and disappears into a private solitude,
as I do, unable to share them
in our sorrow, which delights us.

It amazes each generation
how life speeds up.
I know it amazes mine.
We clean our closets and file papers
not wanting to be caught unprepared.

We write our memoirs
every detail:
hot sand at the beach
lifting her dress,
son's first four steps before toppling over,
the other woman,
the other other woman,
watching our parents die . . .

I wonder where this ends.
Does it go faster and faster
and become a blur
and wink out, a spaceship
jumping into hyperspace?

My life flashes behind my eye,
the entire story compressed into one instant,
suffering and joy revealed to be circular,
beauty and emptiness identical.

Raga

It starts sluggishly
with long chords of contemplation

Life is a drone
and we have time enough for it

It picks up speed and energy
the sitar a full-bodied cloud with silver lining
and the tabla the sun breaking through

The two musicians trade secrets
swap jokes, take risks.
One hurries and the other, frantic,
hurries to catch up

the raga is about a boy running through high grass
to see his first train
about the sheer joy of running and seeing a train

it is about relentless water rising

It is not Western
it is barely human

The taste of the music is in my mouth,
sweet and it is sweet and sour

the estuary fills with tide
the stars wheel outward and leave us.

I died on a Thursday
at 1:30 in the afternoon
at home in Hondo
in bed with my hat on

I called out for beer
and they laughed
It was in May
my time had come

surrounded by people
alone
my fingers considered tiny boxes
fitted inside tiny boxes
my mind
went into a jungle

In May, finally, a stroke
carried me away
in the bed jacket she made for me.

Let's summarize
quickly
before the grass grows any higher.
The situation is not yet dire
we still have our illusions
and our ironies,
our skies show resolve.

No need to panic
We have the daily drip
Let's hit the right notes today
and tomorrow will take care of itself.

Let's say it:
Could have despaired
but didn't.
Let's sing it:
Could have died
in the countryside
but didn't.

So what?
I mean, so, what now?
here in the countryside

Let's whisper

Let's not:
Let's not feel alright
let's not find words for regret or hope
or try to capture small moods any longer.

Blue Hills

Into my heart an air that kills
from yon far country blows;
What are those blue remembered hills,
What spires, what farms are those?

That is the land of lost content,
I see it shining plain,
The happy highways where I went
and cannot come again.

Housman had it wrong;
the blue hills here are not remembered
but are cold and closing in on me,
dark snow-streaked mountains
called the Blood of Christ.

He had it wrong about his childhood too.
He wrote his lines in London
years before he ever visited
his beloved Shropshire.

What I remember is a steep brush-covered hill
behind our house, with rattlesnakes
and the constant threat of wild fire.

And now, what was distant, to the east, is near.
What I fear is not old age or death
but losing my lucidity
– what is left of it.

I start spring chores and find
the apricot has outgrown its bucket,
snows have washed away the path.
I hear mariachi music from two fields over.

  I lied:
  I do fear death
  I say it plain and clear
  and record the voice
  of dying light.

For over a hundred years
we've been told
that when the mountains turn red at sunset
the padres said: Blood of Christ.

Then I read that peasants
in Extremadura believed the waters
from the mountains
give life as Christ gives life.

I don't relate to Catholicism
and think these mountains
are a nearly new geology,
but they are old in the way they move,
a rhythm similar to snakes
and water and music,
rising and falling
– I can almost hear them

and it is true:
   they are agony to me
   and give me life.

A fly buzzed my ear and when I swatted it
it stung the side of my face.
A moment of disbelief
– is that what it is like?

If I could write six or seven poems
in that instant
I would be immortal, before the pain.

Was it Hamlet who said "a sting?"
Or Cleopatra? I'm confused.
Read at Berkeley, a mere scratch, by an asp,
a word comical to undergrads
but as a viper, deadly to the Queen.
A prick? No – that was Mercutio
or Juliet's brother?
Shakespeare's people are mixed up in my mind
like speaking parts of me.

A yellow jacket in my bedroom; I mistook it for a fly.
Without an afterlife its sting is sullen.
A sting and then no pain at all.

I drove east
seeing tractor-trailers packed with steers,
rolling stock snaking across the prairie

I saw a body in the highway
and when I got close,
it flew off in all directions:
ravens eating road kill

I am exiled to this town
to a single room
the hiss of the radiator in the winter
the whirr of the electric fan in the summer

Inland gulls wheel above the stock yards

Exiled here until a train approaches
slows down
and picks me up
smooth and powerful.

I have to be quiet to hear the silence
but the summer is not silent
– plop of a fish jumping
– cicadas in the piñon trees.
I have to be voiceless to hear the whispers
of air in the willows
and the buzz of time passing.
I have to be still and amorous to understand
how much love there is in the world.

I would look into the heart
of this summer of fish and cicadas,
into the heart of this opium dream of life,
into my own heart . . .

The dogs find shade, then bored
wade into the shallows of the river,
its waters nearly nothing compared
to the volume of the Amazon
or the length of the Nile,
this parochial Indian-Hispanic river
that splits the State in two

Nearly nothing
but strong enough to take me like debris
to the city of sin and beyond,
to the mud and oil of the gulf

I would leave them behind,
escape once and for all to freedom.
I can almost taste it.

But this soft-spoken river does not really want me.

Sitting next to the Atalaya ditch
which is flowing fast as old age,
I hear the cry of a bird
that sounds like a hippo grunting,
another like a machine not oiled.
I am not going anywhere,
it is a hot dry day.

Another bird sounds like an echo across water.
I can't locate any of them
and don't know what has agitated them.
It can't be me.
I am still.

1

1

Is this the end? My gut sticking out
and hair falling out,
nothing but modern medicine
between me and oblivion?
Who would have thought
it would be this sweet?

2

Three doctors tell me
I have a year to live,
a year to understand
what is important and possible.

Love ends
Love is all that matters.

In my wild years between marriages
I understood some things
about a world denied to married men,
I understood that lust without loyalty
appeals to certain women
who would use me in ways that I use them,
that sex is all there is
and nothing survives it.

And yet I have survived it
and am here, home, back in Hondo.

First frost freezes the water in the dog dish
and cracks the thermostat, defective mercury.

The jack-o'-lantern sags, looking more depressed
than scary. We carved it again this year
although no ghost or wonder woman ever comes
to our house on the outskirts of the village.

Winter is coming with its first snow
and I wait quietly, not afraid.
I once dreaded it but now
it is just another season,
the one that follows fall
and precedes spring.

Just another season, with its early dark
and freezing dawns and days that follow days . . .

I am astonished that the only thing
required of me now is to remember
and to record what I remember
. . . seeing my sister sitting on the stairs
drunk, like our mother,
with a glazed look on her face
. . . and in the movie theater
pushing a sweeper across the commercial carpet
which is khaki-colored to hide the New Mexican mud.

Who was it who registered
the gray light on the bay
and the cool damp air
so sharply that fifty years later
he remembers their textures?
Although I recall the smell of fog
and the remote moans of foghorns
I don't know for sure that it was me.

In California
I lived in an orchard
in a shack where migrant workers
left behind tin cans and Mexican comic books.

I sat perched in a window
with the Roman plain spread below
listening to scratchy Prokofiev
on a tiny phonograph.

In Ghana I saw a coffin on wheels,
in the shape of a fish with a big mouth
as if it had swallowed the corpse
and with big eyes to see where it was going.

These places, lodged in cells
I thought had died, return
as memories ignited by the smells
of lemon blossoms
and a road repaired with tar
and diesel fumes from buses and trucks.

Proust knew, each place and time,
each moment, holds within its heart
the specifics of a past
and whispers of a future.

I fill my pen with blood
and let it drip drop
by drop.
This is what I live for now,
when the ink of mother's blood
is dried and ground into a paste
and dissolved with alcohol
and sinks into the page,
and later, the invisible ink
surfaces as poems
when time is shined on them.

They are nesting in the hard-drive
and its fledglings, flash-drives.
What happens if they are fifth rate,
if they end up in the trash
dying like the songs of larks in a storm,
what happens then?
Are loves and lamentations extinguished?
Do skies still shine and deserts bloom?

The floors are shiny
and the windows as clean as they are going to be
but the house is full of flies.

The dog hairs are mostly off the sofa,
toilet gleams and dishes washed and put away
but the house still smells.

The guests arrive to find
that everything is shipshape
but we have sailed away.

Asterion

One fresh morning in May my daughter
and I went to the Heraklion Museum of Minoan art
and gazed at the frescos of boys and girls
vaulting over the backs of bulls.

What are they doing? she asked

No one knows for sure. Some say it's man's way
of appeasing the powers that rule our lives,
others that it is a mystic marriage between . . .

Look! [almost a command] The girls are playing,
they are playing with the bull.

At first light we had rolls and butter and bitter coffee
and caught the early bus to Knossos
and wandered through the reconstructed courtyards and rooms
guided by a girl-guide in a crisp blue suit
and an orange streak in her Cretan hair.

In the last room of the tour, my daughter asked her

What lies behind that bricked-up door?

A tunnel, leading to a palace beneath the palace.
Here is how it happened.
Poseidon made an all-white bull that gleamed in daylight
and Pasiphaë, Queen to Minos, daughter of the Sun,
took one look and fell in love
and she told Daedalus (a Greek) to make a hollow cow
and he who loved the Queen and could refuse her nothing
made it with a wooden frame and wooly hides

and an opening in the back for bulls
and it happened just as she imagined,
the bull approached and was aroused and mounted her
to the satisfaction of them both

and later she gave birth to a large baby
she named Asterion which means the starry one
and whom she loved as a mother loves her son
and a cow loves her calf
and proudly showed the King what she had done
and he afraid the mobs would think the boy a monster
asked the clever Craftsman
(who never rejected a commission)
to build a domicile beneath the palace
with many corridors and gates
and complicated gardens to house his stepson,
who grew to have the body of a well-wrought man
and the head of a bull with sharp-tipped horns
so beautiful that Ariadne and Phaedra,
the daughters of the Queen,
asked the Technocrat (flattered by their confidence in him)
to provide them with a thread to lead them
to the star-blessed one
and Asterion was so happy for their company
he raced around with them through all the twists
and turns of his hidden home
and was both brother and lover to them both.

You know, I said to Sara over dinner, the story
by the guide is not the way I heard it.

I know, she said, but I like her version better
than the horrible one of imprisonment and death.
Did you notice, Dad, the ring in her nose?
What, I wonder, does that mean?

Plazuela

Iron ore-cart filled with flowers in bloom,
a fountain with three basins
each one lower and larger than the one above.
Am I in a small plaza in Mexico or in a dream?

A black bird sits in the highest basin
grabbing water in its beak
and throwing it on her own head
like a mourner throwing dust on herself.

Plazuela, what a good word
Plazuela San Francisco,
and in the Café Van Gogh's Ear
the interior is decorated
like the painter's house in Arles
but I prefer the outside covered patio.
The waiter is an earnest twelve year old boy.
Comida del dia is chicken soup,
a mound of sculptured rice,
stale bread, enchiladas, potatoes, a piece of chicken,
and a piece of cake, for $3.80.

Carnations bloom in the ore cart
but it is hard to enjoy them
knowing that Indians
pushed the carts up steep tunnels,
first as slaves, then after freedom
as wage-slaves.

A young woman sets up a row of easels
to display her paintings.
Black hair, bare arms, cut-off jeans
revealing long legs and wide calves:
moving like a doe. It is she, my wife
as she was forty years ago, my love.

Does she see me or does she see
an old man devoid of attraction?
I see myself, a pauper of imagination
unable to mythologize myself
and unable to stop mythologizing myself.

Clouds gather
I am startled
I thought the blue morning would last.
I have an odd thought: that before I know it
I will be back in my chair in Arroyo Hondo
overlooking the orchard and river
lamenting much and dreaming of the time I spent
in Guanajuato outside Van Gogh's Ear.

Thunder groans – air cools
I have a choice:
to rush back and beat the rain
or wait it out here, in "my" plazuela

then the wind that precedes the rain
sweeps the plaza clear of people
except the girl with the paintings
who bangs a tambourine and breaks
into a Tarascan song about singing to the singing frogs.

I smell the rain before it comes
and then it comes
wet, black, noisy
for twenty minutes.

Afterwards another smell,
something ripe almost rotting,
the plaza fills with people,
children at play and a peanut vendor,
three tourists with guide books,
a couple with a baby in a stroller
and a dozen pigeons pecking at something
the rain knocked off the tree.
The stones have stopped steaming
and are glistening in the sunlight.

By the pool

Black hair hangs in a braid
to her shoulder blades,
hips covered by a black bikini,
she stands, poised to dive
into the public pool.
Once an object of desire,
now not even an object of tenderness.
What can I do with her but stare

joined by a second
girl? teen? young woman?
I can't tell their ages anymore.
They have legs and I have eyes
to possess their youth
and be them,
not this old seething thing

and now there are three
and they dive together,
three splashes,
and race up the pool
to no conclusion –
it's silliness not winning.

I could dive in,
an alien from outer age;
as a youth, I swam two lengths underwater.

One ducks her head
and spreads her legs in a V in the air.
Sixteen! That's my guess.

Isn't it better to speculate
than penetrate?
No. It is second best or third.
They are almost ageless
in their ignorance of what I feel,
they are bent on happiness
and oblivious of time and history.

After they leave,
I swim in their water,
my shadow on the bottom of the pool
is flying.

Susanna and the Elders

It is an old story told in the Bible
to warn the girls and titillate the rabbis.

How old was she? Eleven, fifteen, twenty-one?
I imagine her thirteen with hips like a boy
and budding breasts
because that is what old men want,
a girl, but not a child.

I used to see them as desiccated and feeble
but now I know they are sixty-eight or so
with bellies and gray hair, still capable
but beginning to be strange with age.

One of them wants to look
more than he wants to love,
another to penetrate every orifice
orifice after orifice and never stop.
A third is almost indifferent;
he would prefer a boy.

Stevens has her cool in green water,
but clothed in rhetoric,
his girl is more music
than a living breathing woman.

Artemisia Gentileschi has it right,
paints her with wide hips but not excessive,
a fresh brunette who attracts
the light and their lecher eyes,
a wife who thinks she knows the ways of love
because she loves her husband's soft black hair,
his voice, his chest . . .

180

and she loathes the elders
and is repulsed by the lewdness of their lust
and the things they say, first behind their hands
and then to her.

The Bible story is a court case – "she says, they say" –
until she trips them up
with some Talmudic nonsense
but that is not the part people remember.
It is the looking that excites us, and the being seen.

I create my own Susanna
fresh from the desert,
black hair and dusky skin and soft gray eyes
who throws her clothes off
and lowers herself into the water
that is cool against her thighs,
naked as only a woman can be
and sings an antique Hebrew song:
wife, woman, a little wild, even crazy
and spied upon, gives the evil eye to them
and struts home through the palm trees
proud, faithful, eager for her husband.

I would write a poem about her,
how she steps into the pool in the heat of midday,
birds singing in the trees, a breeze lifting her hair,
and she splashes water upward on her breasts
and wipes it downward off her hairless belly
and moans with pleasure,
not realizing how many painters and poets
in the Western world are watching her
and figuring how to make her.

Warm wind from the east
carries the cries of ravens
but no rain

We wait every day
and we listen
we do listen
we hear hammer blows
and screaming ravens

We hear wind
from noon to sundown
It comes in gusts
We hear it
then we don't

we hear tap tap tap of hammers
and the buzzing of flies

we didn't listen like this
when we were young

we see the wind
a plastic chair blown over

the dog barks
and trots
up the driveway
so we look
and see the dirt road

if we listen
we can hear the weeds growing
and the wind
we are waiting for rain

we think
with rain
words will come

It is July
and thunderstorms
surround us

we see them
on the mountains
to the east
and on the moon-like plains
to the west

the wind blows
and the sky clouds over
but these are dry thunderstorms
thunder without lightning

then thunder and lightning
without rain

We look at each other

we long ceased listening to each other
but we still look at each other
our looks like dry thunderstorms.

All fall
the cottonwoods were full of ravens
but today, they are gone.

I sit outside in the cold.
It is the shortest day
but not the darkest.
The sky is bright and clear.

my father died at 9:30 this morning

The Filipino housekeeper found him in bed
pumped full of morphine, stiff,
his knees drawn up.
She went into the kitchen and said to his wife
"The doctor has taken his last breath."

I was with him two days ago.
With his false teeth out,
his mouth was a gaping hole.
I rubbed his head and said
"Dad, it's okay; it's going to be okay."

The shortest day
under a blue sky
♫nothing but blue sky
Smoke rises from the village.

"scarce seven hours,"
Donne wrote of St. Lucie's Day.
"Earth drinks a balm
and I am every dead thing."

Dec. 21, 2005

The door is creaking
and I hear city hall
I hear the sounds of the souk in midday
I suppose it is my poor hearing
and the confusion of old age
and too much solitude

I admit that solitude
is the drug I most crave

The creaking door
sounds like people chattering,
like faint Corelli

Then all falls silent,
the afternoon light
is falling and accumulating.

After a brush with barbed wire
I glance at my hand
and see blood running between my fingers
in a glowing rivulet.

Insect bites, calf caught on a nail,
puncture from a willow branch:
the world breaks into me
and does me harm for all to see,
each wound a question.

I rip the scabs off,
scratch the insect bites,
open up the wounds
and refuse an answer.

It is February
a tricky month.
Green grass growing
under last year's grass.
By ten it gets warmer
from thirty to forty degrees
in a rising tide of warmth
that unfreezes the dirt.
Five obituaries in this week's paper
tell the story
ages 67, 73, 51, 82, 71.
Walking on the mushy road
around three the air already begins to cool
and the ground to freeze.

Is poetry possible in any season,
in summer stupor and fall heartache?
Can I find something to say
when snow blocks the road and I am housebound?
Can I keep it simple in spring
when sensuality overwhelms me?

Is this the end,
when I don't distinguish winter from fall,
when I am joyful in January and sad in July
and all the seasons feel like seasons from my past?
When I lose myself and in the process lose us four?
Then there is nothing else to lose and I am lost.

Or is it a new season, a fifth season?
Isn't that what I have been waiting for?
One with neither birth nor death
but vacant weather and silence,
the pen filled with dust slips from my hand,
the sheet of paper slides off my lap . . .

Touched by the morphine drip of days
I would like to say a few honest words
about my moods
    that is not possible
Of course that is not possible
words themselves are dishonest

Then about my nights
sitting outside
with the moon
without words
just wind on my face.
    But without words
    can I have the moment?

Two in the morning
thin clouds blowing across the moon
that is sailing through the clouds
fast, like a fast ship

On another night
I bathe in the warmth of the sun
reflecting off the moon

On a third night
I see the moon over the southern hills
just a sliver, elegant, modest
like a thin slice of lemon

two, three four moons
that reflect my selves
without words.

De Montherlant's Chaos et la Nuit, about a prickly and isolated Spanish anarchist self-exiled in Paris for twenty years, is one of the bleakest books ever written. The author was a misanthrope, disillusioned and bitter in uninteresting ways, an anti-Quixote. He was attacked and beaten for his pedophilia in Paris in 1968 and lost the sight in one eye. Toward the end of his life, he was almost entirely blind. A desperate suicide, he took a cyanide pill and then, to be sure, shot himself in the head.

Everyone is bored, the shadows are bored,
pick up the phone
and discover a dial tone.
Mailbox is empty.
Nothing is trying to reach me.

Exhausted and unshaven in a Paris park
I watch as mothers ignore their children to flirt with men.
I see an old man in the wine store, his gaze downward,
his fly unzipped. The clerks notice too,
indifferent witnesses to the shuddering flame.

How mock those who choose to live?
Who still feel lust?
How scorn the successful
or question those who have illusions;
they are the future.
How doubt the enlightened
who are forever.

It was once enough to watch
as words flowed to the page,

but I am tired of words,
words spoken at me,
words written down with me in mind,
and most of all, my own words.

How many times have I promised myself to end it.
At 22, 35, 63, 70. Swollen with age,
losing teeth and hair; I could list the loses.

"A tiresome person" my friend says
who still has things to do.
"You've lived," he says, "you've loved,
why would you want to die?"
I explain, it is not my past
but my present that compels me.
I fear that all is over: plays, novels, travel, lust, boys.

Another friend, a Jewish moralist,
maintains I simply want control
as always, even over death.

These friends, my voices, have it right.
I want things to be clean and in their place.
I want the end to come before the end.
I want people to feel pity for me.
I want revenge.

In short, it has been a bad day,
its only virtue that it ends.
Wind creeps under my shirt and fondles me obscenely
and no matter how desperate
no boy is going to find me desirable.
I am going to ask the woman who cuts my hair
to cut it short. short as for a man going into battle.

What a bore, old age.
Our feuds grow old with us,
our self-feuds even older.
Each man in time exists in time;
insipid thoughts and bloated hearts
are equal in the eyes of fate.

Death tattoos its contradictions on us,
red becoming rust,
regret becoming rage.
Others have experienced this
and survived.
I will revive
and marry a rich woman.
Or do I want to die?
which death is real?

Old if not toothless
hairless earless sightless
or just plain heartless.
Don't scent the air
that rots between us.
It's not worth it to me
him, you, a cripple
in spirit and in fact.
The sound of what one thought
was real bright clear,
why do it, each day why
struggle to love and act in love.
Why grow old to find that we are old
on the horizon of nothing.

And yet (that word still haunts me)
I still care about bird's cry
and the sunrise rough and driven . . .

Reading in the sun

They said it already,
in Marlowe-speak and Yeats'
voice seeping into mine
and mine unmanned and old
ashamed that I have placed
my trust in old books and oblivion.

And then Machado's voice
that says Soria is air
Soria is sorrow

and I write my Solitudes.

January first:
love people more
and the dogs less,
lose weight
and let my imagination loose
in the valley of my imagination.
Adhere to three principles:
        clarity, economy, architecture.
Then I will be the final me,
the one who has nothing to lose
exception my resolutions.

My father took me deer hunting,
taught me how to shoot a .30-30
but I feigned illness, stayed behind
to inhale the sweet perfume of loose hay
and stalk crows with my single-shot .22

Doctors, artists and ranch hands
hooked bucks to the barn,
cleaned barrels with gauze
soaked in slippery gun oil,
told tales of red-hot brunettes.

Old age beginning now
and Jimmy understanding old images
of hunting and hunters
who thought that killing
was a way of loving life.

It's a comfort to know
the Etruscans disappeared
and the Greeks were unable to sustain their thought
and beasts disappear
and plants and then the planet
and then the star we call the sun will
and I too, not hung from a high branch
or in a bar in Gallup
where Navajo whores drink me into the floor
or beyond the kelp in the swells,
but here at the end of the long process
of flourishing a pen in the Hondo valley.

According to Zeno we halve halves forever
so there is nothing left to live for.
A warm fall day revives me for an hour
but then I think of January
and realize seasons dictate.
I was never free
and never less free than now
living a half-life in half the time.

But reading the Sicilian Empedocles
I return to sanity
  and accept that air is my element
    water my design
        fire my spirit
          and earth my destiny.

To look at them,
the cloudy sky
and snow-streaked field,
you would think they were dead
but they are alive
with the sly promise of spring.

Shirt open
sleeves rolled up like a sailor
on the open sea
or a farmer on the first day of planting
I greet each dawn
as the sun rises higher every day.
Wake up
New Mexico is calling
These clouds are dancing
and show the way.

There were three of them
like gigantic mosquitoes.
I heard them before I saw them,
then they blocked out the sun,
three of them from the south, in tandem,
rotors roiling the air,
imperial and sinister.
I gave them a look of scorn
and sat down and wrote this "poem"
and knew what my wife and son won't admit:
they are not watching us.

At five
the wind dies down –
time to feed the dogs,
the dusk in Paris is purple
and at sea, day turns to night

I eat alone, indifferent
to sweet and salty, sour and bitter
and don't succumb to the hour

a five hurricane is the most destructive

the yard is mushy with snow
and wet leaves,
the sky is egg white,
I do the dishes
and wash a woolen cap
that fell into the mud

NPR says a Nigerian woman
has been released after five years
in prison for murdering her daughter

and I remember closing five fingers
around a woman's throat

Time for Lorca's friend to die
a las cinco de la tarde

My mother had her first drink at five.

Listening to Dvořák's cello concerto
thinking it will resurrect feelings
I had when I loved music
and a particular girl,
the strings and horns expressing
full-throated emotions I barely recognize.

I go outside and outside is empty
of Dvořák, of his rhetoric and feeling.
Gray ripples of light
shine on the dust.
The sun burns the wind
the wind cleans the earth

I spent time in Dvorak's world
and prefer mine of sun and wind

I spent time in the real world
but prefer mine of dust and light.

Open the window and latch it open
light comes in carried on the air.

On impulse walk to the apple tree
to see if the buds survived the frost.

The young do not suspect
the subtle pleasures of the old
and how they sustain us.

The path through the green grass, for instance,
is nearly invisible at noon,
but at dawn, it shows up clearly as a shadow.

It goes from the house across the grass
and wavers slightly
before it reaches the orchard.

I didn't try to understand its significance
until one dawn, groggy from a sleeping pill,
I saw it defined by the early light,
sinuous and deliberate,
a record of our routine.

Snow straying across the front of the house,
then a swelling wind that clears the sky,
later a burst of raw warmth.
The weather is uncertain
and the future is unclear.
Our best chance is to build
a sanctuary out of our routines,
to be with familiar things
in this changeable hour.

1

Sitting on a bench munching my morning bagel
I watch old Chinese men and women fast-walking around the park
and doing tai-chi on the grass.

Close to me, two young homeless men are picking their toenails
in the fall sunshine.

> "I'm not hungry but I will be later."
> "I got so fucked up last night."
> "It happens."

A black man, his head tilted to the sun, sleeping, perhaps dreaming.
A young woman sitting on a bench,
just sitting, no book, no fidgeting.

. . . at nine, a few bangs of the bell from the Washington Square church
and smells of cigarette smoke and car exhaust.

2

Sitting at a table outside the Café Puccini,
classical music seeping from the interior but it is not Puccini.
Lunch arrives, omelet with chives, then coffee
while I read the poetry of Cesare Pavese.
A bar across the street:
"Happy hour 4 pm to 8 pm. 28 beers on tap."
The barmaid is sitting on a chair on the sidewalk
reading the newspaper. Behind her,

the open door of the cavern tempts me
because I would be the first customer,
my eyes slowly adjusting to the dark.

3

If I moved here, I would establish a routine:
writing in a room, go to the library
and take the same route back to my desk.
I would occasionally eat dinner out,
pick a seat next to the window so I could watch the street scene,
the Chardonnay and the sharp cream sauce of spaghetti carbonara
would bring back our nights in Rome eating at sidewalk restaurants,
the four of us, me, my wife, our son and daughter
reliving the events of the day, the trip, our life together.

A moody day, in which
I sit outside with a notebook,
a cold June day
that reminds me of another cold June day
thirty-five years ago
when Phaedra and I were cutting willows
out of the acequia,
clouds bottom-heavy
stretching off into the next county.

It is strange
that this cold day
reminds me of a time
so distant, sunk in routine labor,
not suspecting that I would remember
the sensation as hail fell,
sharp things striking our faces and arms.
The dogs looked at us
and the cats disappeared.
The hail drove us inside
and the chickens into their coops,
dogs under the table,
ducks into their house
which did not protect them from snakes.

Alone three days,
a man approaches wearing gloves

> You've come to kill me
> Yes
> Sent by she who loves me
> Yes
> What did she promise you – land? love?
> Some of both
> She'll keep her word
> She will!

And he melts away
in the light air
a phantom of my murderous heart.

The Proper Distance

About suffering, the Old Masters
may never have been wrong
but they didn't always agree.
Ovid for instance says the fisherman,
ploughman and shepherd looked up
and wondered what specks these were,
men or gods, flying through the sky,
while Bruegel's fisherman is fishing,
ploughman ploughing and shepherd herding:
fathers all, they must work.
It is Auden, modern master,
who says they see the falling boy
and turn away, having better things to do.

Ovid's is a full account,
of a fruitful island of bulls and acrobats,
a boy laughing while he thumbs the soft wax
and a father, fabulous inventor,
scolding the boy and kissing him
and saying don't fly too low
or the waves will soak the wings
and weigh you down
or too high, the sun will melt the wax.

Sailors sail on but look
who stopped to see:
Ovid borrowing from old myths,
Bruegel with palette and brush
overlooking field and sea,

and Auden, in a tweed jacket,
gazing at a painting in the Musee des Beaux Arts.
And I am writing about them
and you are reading this.
Where do we stand?
What is the proper distance from the suffering
of the boy who staggered in the sky
and from the father who heard his boy's cry
smothered by the sea
and wept in anger/love
and circled helplessly
and finally flew on to Sicily
and his labyrinth of grief.

The End

and the credits began to roll to haunting music,
the cast, producers, director . . .
those whose souls belong to SAG,
as I sat stunned by all the mayhem, detonated cars, strafed crowds
and the betrayals: the needle in the neck,
the odorless fumes leaked into the bedroom,
it all made sense but didn't, recalling the chase through the souk
and the caravan of six black Navigators headed for Wadi Aish
in the Empty Quarter to the cries of muezzins from the minarets

and the credits scrolled
best boy, hair stylist, foley editor,
stunt double, stunt driver, rigging grip . . .
Ministers met, couriers departed and didn't arrive,
the sheik's man whispered Maktoob, it is written,
and Mossad nodded, saying the inevitable is inevitable,
so more met violence, some shot, some drowned,
some done in by poisoned aperitifs.
When she glimpsed the obvious and ominous truth
that the bomb had exploded <u>inward</u> through the house
and killed his double, the state secret
became her personal secret of flesh and deception.
roto artist, model maker, sound mixer, painter, wrangler,
matchmove artist, dialect coach, carpenter, driver . . .
I had not thought it took so many to make a movie.

And of course the Americans were implicated watching from space
and the Chinese listening and decoding into Mandarin
and the perfidious Russians and their poisons

and the militia that took its name from verse 57
and still the credits rolled
chefs, on-set tutors, color assistant, payroll,
casting UK, casting Pakistan . . .

there were no bows or flowers,
only names flickering on the screen
like names written by a scribe in the book of dust
while the scope of the conspiracy widened, cross and double cross,
the regime changed but nothing changed,
a train derailed in Poland, a blast in Bogota,
and in Paris, the assassination of a diplomat
who carried in his briefcase plans to weaponize imports.

colorist, set dresser, assistant script girl, matte painter, stitcher,
and then locations: *La Paz, Dakar, Krakow, Amman, Recife, Akaba -*
and the swelling music helped me understand
that behind this artifice the truth is simpler than I realized,
that the story ends, even the credits finally end.

This tale of light and shadow concluded I got up and left,
walked out through the well-lit lobby into the theater of the night.

I hear voices
melodious
monotonous
not mine
but for me

I listen
and they fade
why
is no longer important

I am ready to descend
into some truth
that resides in me
and in the world

increasingly deaf
I hear voices
without words
I hear voices
that sound like waves
rolling in and eating away the coast

[voices] better that I do not
understand the words
Their flow
matters more

and then
I would be sober
while drunk

and then
drunk while sober

create
then let go

and clouds
and waves

I would end there
in the sea

and then
and then

I love a woman,
    I love our son and daughter
        but even love passes

        in the evening the stars rise
        a simple actual event

        and set

        say to them go
        go on without me

        go –

and I am caught in the flow
    bobbing shining
        breathing air
            then water

A siren in the city is one thing,
so frequent to be nothing,
but a siren in the country is another.
At first it is a faint sound from the highway
that could be a gypsy singing or a lullaby

What is it to me?
I am old and detached,
the siren is just a minor
reminder of mortality

but closer, it becomes a shriek
of someone really suffering
from a fire, bullet, crash or stroke

and ending badly in the ER
or hospice or the morgue

and then it climbs the hill towards town
and fades forever.

Cholla

They live here just as we do but apart
on hillsides, some as tall as children,
indomitable and dangerous.
We pretend not to notice them
but they were here before us
and will be after we are gone.
They have shallow roots and are easy to dig out
but we leave them alone and they leave us alone.
We fear falling into them because of their spines.

Do I aspire to be one of them,
here forever, untouchable?

I sit at the blue table, my Mediterranean,
drinking a rum and coke.
A wasp hovers around the glass
and climbs down the inside of it
and starts to swim.

Then crawls up the inside
and hoists itself to the lip and sits there in a stupor.
It begins walking around the edge
and then down the outside of the glass
and falls to the table, exhausted or drunk.
After a while it flies away.

On another day, sitting in the shade of the olive tree
listening to Javanese music
I find a fire ant floating in my glass of red wine.
I try to imagine what alcohol
is doing to her nervous system.
Will it blunt her aggressiveness?
Will she forget her sisters and the Queen?
Regret her life of labor?
Or be an angry drunk? Or sentimental?
Besotted by new sensations and feelings,
will sorrow overwhelm her?

I fish her out
and put her on the ground to stagger home,
confused but not ashamed,
to try to tell the others what – if anything –
she has learned and understands.

1

In April we moved your ashes
from the stony hillside
to the orchard by the river
into a patch of ground
beneath an old cedar tree,
its red and gray bark
like the stripes of a dress.
It first grows right
and then straight up and forks
into two and rising
forks again up twenty feet
into the claws of its leaves.
What does it know?
How do you know?

In mid-May I plant wild grasses and flowers
and listen to the river
and the wind in the cedar
and consider your ashes
in a gold-tinted box.
I listen for you
but you are past speaking.
In the circle of your shadow
I ask myself,
do you distort me the way
the sun distorts time and space?
Is this a shrine or sanctuary
or cemetery?
Will I be scattered
or buried like you with grave goods?

2

I tie a line to a watering can
and throw it downstream
where it floats and then fills
and then sinks.
I pull it to me, large fish,
and walk the path
and water the grass and flowers.

Three, four times I toss the can
and pull it in
filled with something living
and walk fourteen steps
up the stony path
and water the grass
and the red geraniums and gold marigolds.

3

Late summer, pop and blues and string quartets
on my MP3 player the size of my thumb,
Fats Domino finding his thrill on Blueberry Hill,
I was born by the river sings Sam Cooke,
things are going to change
meaning for blacks but for me too,
are already changing.
Shimmering gamelan
sweet and sour raga
growl of cello and flight of violin,
the strings and horns

billowing me into the future.
Now there is reggae and I am
out of the chair and moving shirtless
under the line of soaring cottonwood trees,
clumsy on the ancient path,
tiny yellow flowers at my feet
with spiky petals
that survive without rain
rooted below the wind
adapted to this dirt

then really dancing
knees high
sweetness of the sun on my chest
and music and the grass growing
and the path blazing
and the cedar tree with its branches
waving like arms.

4

In the winter
I sit with you,
lying under your blanket of snow.
It seems like a long time ago
that I sat writing and didn't write,
that I moved in a joyful shuffle
that became a dance
over the yellow flowers.
Although words are inadequate
to the feelings I bring
to you, to me, to all of us,
I write this, not grieving
or celebrating, but filled with love
at peace at last in the winter light.

As if all the moments up to now
were stagecraft
and only now authentic

As if sick with lies
and only now well

I survived the four hundred blows of youth
and I am going to survive
the four thousand caresses of old age.

Sitting outside on a clear night
I see constellations
not of stars but of spaces between stars:
Dog's Face, Beer Truck, the Phallus
and waking, remember my child's
blue book of constellations.

Sitting in the sun
I doze off and dream of the Girl
whose Limbs are Hairless,
the Bridge and the Bear
and waking, release regrets
and remember an old man's dream
of a Simple Dance.

I was crazy to think that my mother was signaling to me
by flashing sunlight through the palm tree in La Paz
but it felt good and made me happy,
at least at first: then sorrow.

I didn't really believe, did I?

Here, under the silver poplar, it doesn't happen
unless there is a faint breeze to move the leaves
and create the flashing effect, the leaves
that are green on one side, silver on the other.

When did it start, this sorrow,
Cordoba in 1960
or in the Upland lemon grove the year before
or 1956 when I discovered there were other boys
in her life (and several men)
or even earlier, realizing like most adolescents
there is no hope or in Taos in 1952, age 12,
when something happened within me or in my world?

When did I realize
the progression of souls has no meaning?

Bach understands these questions
Shostakovich has something to say about it
Otis Redding on his dock
Scott Joplin is mumbling at his piano
having embedded his sorrow
in musical phrases, progeny of decay.
The poets too, all of them have ways of looking

at this. I go inward past Rilke to Machado,
past Machado to find my sorrow
and then find words for sorrow,
then past words-for-sorrow
to a white page

  and a white page
  cannot write on a white page.

Half blind I am blinded
by the sun flashing
through a tree

Nuclear blast softened by leaves,
time semaphoring to me
of light and love

I am living
with blood on my fingers

I am dying with light
flashing in my eye

        wait for me.

Walking in the hills, the dogs and I, in March,
we come upon an umbrella, and under it,
a middle-aged woman at her easel
facing the mountains far to the east.
What does one say to a woman
who thought she was alone with her art?

Hello
Hello
Beautiful day
Yes it is

Polite speak, neutral, and I glance at the painting
where she has depicted the entire range,
snow still on the highest peaks,
lower ridges bare,
the whole dipping and rising
like the undulant waves of the sea
and at the base of the mountains,
smoke rising from a village.

It is powerfully tranquil.
And I want to say

You are tranquil too
out here

In the middle of the night
I imagine the conversation going differently.

Is it possible you are the Elizabeth
I flirted with after my divorce?
Have you read Cezanne's biography?

and looking at the mountains I say

I too am aligned with their rhythm and their line,
and the village, that is where I live.

It was on the evening news:
an alcoholic heroin addict sleeping in a box
with the manufacturing code stamped inside
was discovered by a reporter to have been famous.
His face was ravaged, he was missing most of his teeth,
he had lost his family and friends to horse and rum.
He had no use for his body and no memory of his mind.
Even his enemies were blurs.
But he had been a renowned broadcaster in Cleveland
and had retained his deep, vibrant voice.

They cleaned him up, put him in rehab, paid for a dentist,
and he made the rounds of the talk shows.
They gave him a job and an apartment with beige carpets.

He dreamed he was running swiftly
and woke up and was young again.
On another night, he woke up aroused
having dreamed that he and she . . .

But he missed being drunk and high and returned to it.
He enjoyed being desolate, but it was more than that.
He wanted the euphoria of oblivion.
He wanted that vacant gaze, not inward,
there was nothing inside, not outward,
there was nothing out there.
His goal, his desire:
to gaze on nothing forever.

It is blue with thin red stripes,
thick enough to block the heat
but thin enough to let the light through.
I don't know why the beach umbrella moves me
as it does. I never spent a summer with a frieze of girls;
but having set it up to shield me from the desert sun
I feel a strong emotion connected to the way
the air stirs the edges of the canvas
and makes them sway

and then a memory is ignited
by the way the light shines
through the thin material:
the Jersey shore, age 14,
there to celebrate my grandparents'
50th anniversary
when a girl said she loved me.

Am I remembering correctly,
looking from the sand
past the waves to where a plane of blue
meets a plane of blue?
I wonder if the beach is not imaginary,
a construct of my reading,
nostalgia for a place I never was.

I ran across the hot sand to an umbrella
and lay there under it listening to the sea
while I waited for her to take a break
from being a maid in the hotel.

On her day off, we chased little birds
that ran before the surf and lay for hours
on the sand and twined our fingers
and kissed gently; overhead,
a prop plane pulled a banner
proclaiming her hotel.
For different reasons
we didn't say our ages.

I'd read Lady Chatterley's Lover
but didn't know how to kiss;
and she – I don't know what she'd seen
or known – only that she loved me.
She proved it daily, as our kisses
grew more heated, our hands began to stray.

On my last night, she said we'd meet
at midnight, on the beach,
and I thought this is it, we will do it,
and when I told my aunt
I was going to the end-of-summer party
my aunt said no, I wasn't.

The next day, on the plane at Idlewild,
the girl came on the tarmac
and followed the plane
waving and mouthing that she loved me.

At prep school, I got presents from her,
a pen, a wallet, a watch,
and love letters filled with x-s and o-s
and her age: twenty-one.

I finally wrote her, that I had a girlfriend,
it wasn't true, exactly
but I was afraid, confused.

Only now, under an umbrella
with edges flapping in the desert air,
do I feel compassion for what troubled her
and who she may have been
and what she may have felt
for an ignorant boy
too tall and sensual for his years.

Between my junior and senior year
I lived in my mother's garage
and across the street, a woman hanging
sheets and pillowcases
and the shirts and pants and underwear
of a man, a woman and boys and girls,
six lines of laundry,
a brunette, not much older than me,
a Mrs. Fields, my mother said
with just the slightest lift of her lip.

A hot summer, I lay in the room over the garage
and read St. Exupery's Wind, Sand and Stars,
Manzoni's The Betrothed, and listened to a tiny radio,
Herb Alpert's The Lonely Bull
and Linda Ronstadt's Different Drummer.
A few birds were chirping, a car passed on the country road,
and I looked out and saw her in the yard
hanging laundry and feeding hens, a handsome woman
in a short-sleeved dress that revealed her thin arms
and hid her large bust.

Hi, my name is Jim. I'm living across the street

From a height of weariness, she gave me a look that said:

I know you college boy,
and I ain't saying you ain't goodlooking
but I ain't having it and you ain't getting any
so go on home

In the evenings I sat with my mom
who listened to Scott Joplin's rags
and rattled the thin pages of the Times Literary Supplement
and let the ice melt in her glass of scotch
and let her cigarettes burn down.

Mrs. Fields and I could both hear an owl hooting in the night
and the rooster's cry in the morning.
At dawn I climbed to the roof of the garage
and looked at the last stars
and the slice of ocean shining in the west.

A second visit to the clothes lines,
the grass thinly surviving the children's feet,
a rabbit in a hutch (for meat)
a rooster and his hens (for eggs)
and panties and bras not in sight.
I learned a little: first name Donna,
her husband spent the week in San Fernando
repairing city buses,
two boys and a girl away at grandma's,

and I told her that I was back from Italy, majoring in Italian lit.,
I played basketball my freshman year;
she listened patiently and then, cracker grammar gone,
another look, that said:

> Can't you tell, I've got my doubts,
> I'm really tired and the world is rough
> and I am rough;
> and here's the dirt: my belly is covered with stretch marks,
> so please stop making eyes at me,
> you'll live a lot longer

He played the piano in brothels, my mother said of Joplin,
and died at 49 of syphilis.
The summer got hotter, my room unbearable,
I could smell the road melting
and the dust on the avocado trees.
The sea was a long way away.

A third time, I saw an engine hanging
from the branch of a tree
and she had put on lipstick
and this look had a note of sadness:

> Don't get me wrong, I understand you want a woman who'll
> make you a man,
> but I'm not in the market for a boy who loves,
> and furthermore, you'll be leaving soon
> so – go.

My heart breaks for my son
not least because he is drifting away from me.

There is something Asian in his soul,
detached and sad,
and I, old, once a sensualist
am left behind.

Each soul not a star, not a black hole,
not a stone with a fish in it,
but a flake of snow in March
landing in a green sea.

Have to be quiet to hear words not yet spoken,
the ones that come on the air "out of the blue"
Have to be quick to see a firefly
brief as a wink.

Epicurus understood this
and said as much
in simple language:
soul is body
body soul
and at death
they die together.

There is no misunderstanding him:
those who died on Wednesday
are just as dead as Empedocles.

1

What? Words?
My refuge against
decay of nerves
and spongy mind.

What? Words?
Keep them simple
Saxon, short!
Stay on steady ground.

2

Having reached the end of the road,
    I think I will travel.
Finding myself swinging on the end of a rope,
    I think I will fly.

They will find poems embedded in the bark,
hidden in the woodpile like treasures,
buried in the adobe walls,
stamped into the mud in spring,
drawn in the dust
or did I hide them too well?

The ones written in invisible ink,
etched into the table after three glasses of wine,
scratched into the window,
no surface is safe from me,
and the ones written in dried blood
and hidden in the trunk.

They know the words are there,
even the ones written in the Rio Hondo
and carried away,
especially those, for them and about them.

Today, we took a tour of the property
and felt as gnarled as the tree struck by lightning in 1972
and as bleak as the anthill abandoned in 1985,
as dead as the apricot tree that died in the winter of '99
and was cut up for firewood,
as useless as the footbridge that collapsed in 2005.
These deaths defeated us momentarily
but we survived them –
gnarled, bleak, dead, useless
we survived them and thrive.

for Phaedra

It has happened again, the green,
green apple tree, green alfalfa field,
I had forgotten it would happen again.
My heart leaps.

Light flows down and blankets the green
with green as if the light is green, green
filled with green sparks. Even the silence is green.
The world is so exuberant it appears to be in motion.
Stones and the green itself are moving to music.
The day clangs, a ship's bell
but the green here is greener than the sea.
There is no need to hope. It all is!

I sit in the sun like a cancer patient
but with a lot of hair
and strong teeth and powerful hands
a large man but not larger than life

sit as if in a wheelchair
in the windy sunlight
drawing into my lungs the bright air,
my old big heart pumping powerfully

the giant is enjoying the day.

I was slow and sweet,
pre-erotic, adrift in the day
looking around at everything
because everything was interesting.
Where I was, there was light,
light that shines green on the leaf
and red on the flower.

Wordless, how much of me was me then?
Wordless – and now with words
to wonder who I was
- a normal boy oblivious of how oblivious I was,
not understanding I was understanding,
although not innocent, never innocent.

The sensation of light, warmth not quite heat,
boats blurred by a hint of haze, summer of '58.
Running, I ran for what seemed forever.
Swimming, I swam far out as if to Catalina.
It was girls who made me aware of myself
but it is the touch of the air I remember.
She was sensuous
but it is the way the light was part of the air
that I feel again on my skin.

In Los Angeles I watched from the beach
and saw a pattern:
waves come in series, little low ones
and then a series of big ones.

They say to dive under the waves
and come up on the other side.
I swim and when the big wave comes
I dive under it –
it's simple it's exhilarating
and emerge on the other side
in the swells.

They say to dive deep
or a big one will drag you under,
dive almost to the bottom
and come up beyond it, in the green swells.

I dive under the biggest one
because it is safe there
from the roar and violence overhead.

Classic poets reassure us
that oars rise like wings
and rivers flow into the sea

Which will it be,
electric storm in the brain
proliferation of inhuman cells?
– an idle question

A roar but I won't hear it
an agony I won't feel.

The sun rose a little higher today
the last day of the year,
and as usual, I go to bed at eight and as usual
I am wakened at midnight
by the popping of guns in the village.
There is probably a display at the bridge,
sparks falling into the sluggish river,
and in town, municipal fireworks.
On TV, a continuous celebration crawls around the world
beginning in the middle of the Pacific
and moving west through 24 time zones.
People will kiss.

Why this joy, at the passing of a year that featured
rising seas and falling planes and record highs and lows,
the clatter of multi-clips in theaters and schools
and walking bombs and drones that pick out
the bad and the good and the children?
Why this celebration for a single click of the clock?

Time defines us in ways we must accept.
People will love.

This sense of river – I embrace it – I enter it
pretending not to know what it means . . . how it ends . . .
pretending that the loving, the forward motion of it all
and the dying are not related.
     Love, my subject, is inevitable.
         There is only this
              and let's say this is bliss.

ADAPTATIONS, IMITATIONS AND TRANSLATIONS

The fact is, she was drawn to me
and pursued me

I skimmed across the milky lake
the gray sky towered overhead

I trudged up the path
with fish in my sack

We coupled as snakes do
compelled and impersonal

Why do I bring a gift
when it was she who pursued me?

after Lorca

If we had 10,000 years
I say let's spend them fucking
face to face and backwards
Another 20,000
tearing at each other's flesh
We could learn to suck
at all the orifices

Only after one cycle of creation
would we subside to kissing cock and cunt
Another just for kissing
lip to lip

I would celebrate
the way your hips join your legs
the way your buttocks round out your skirt

After a hundred years
I look into your eyes
first one, then the other
Your startled face stills under my gaze
as we vibrate slowly

But we both know
we do not have the time
to orchestrate our lust
to perfection

I can push your skirt up
just so many times
before love mutates
into tenderness or hate

My course hair is getting grayer
and your skin is losing its brightness

Let us acknowledge how heavy
the wind blows
and the river goes
and lie in the tangle of wet sheets
frank and intricate

for I see you flying into eternity
red and bewildered
without me.

after Marvell

My seventieth year had come and gone,
I sat, a solitary man,
above a snowy field and icy river,
two books and a steaming cup
on the round glass table-top

and while I gazed upon the cold white world
my mind lit up, a blaze that brought
the recognition that many have preceded me
and many more will follow
from winter to astonished spring.

apologies to Yeats

After twenty years of debate with myself
I am ready to answer the question:
Is man part of nature?

The answer is
nature does not know how shabby or convoluted
our minds are
nor care how grotesque the body becomes.

The more we resist
the more subtle time's revenge is.

from the Italian

Two lovers
walking slowly through a meadow

"Does our ecstasy seem ancient to you?"
"Very."
Weren't we funny
clinging to each other all the time?"
"It doesn't matter."

"If you could
would you try for it again?"
"What exactly?"

"That happiness! That blueness!"

Two lovers
speeding through a frozen field.

after Verlaine

If you died I would not die
my grief would pass
but this separation seems forever.
I have had no news from the city.
You came into my dream
so you know my longing for you.
Are you dead in my dream or alive?
Across so far, I cannot tell.
You came through the mountain pass;
then, in the trees, turned back.

The setting moon is shining on my bed.
I can almost see your face.
Where are you
the waters are deep
the waters are insane.

To Li Po, from Tu Fu

When my slave tied the chickens up for market
they screamed and struggled.
My wife and father dislike having the chickens eat the ants.

Why should humans side with either ants or chickens?
I tell the slave to untie the chickens.
Leaning against the house,
gazing at the cold river,
I think there can be no end
to the dispute between chickens and ants.

from the Chinese

The boatmen cast loose and unfurled the brightly embroidered sail,
geese flew from the reeds, my friend played the flute and I the guitar.

As we approached the center of the lake
we saw the mountains quivering in the water,
our boat collided with a cliff, the moon swam out of the highest peak.

Suddenly the darkening universe took on a strange color,
the vast stretch of water was breaking like glass.

The spirit of the waters beat its drum.
Perhaps a thunderstorm struck.
After rapid turns of joy and sadness
how long can the illusion of staying young last?

after Tu Fu

Journey North

In the second month of the emperor's reign
I prepared to go north toward home
A degree permitted me to travel
I felt ashamed to accept it
in times as difficult as these.

As we crossed the paddy fields
a bleeding sobbing man broke
from the smoke and stumbled.

In the mountains where ancient carts
have rutted the rocks,
the moon burned the bones of a million men.
Half the population was hurt or broken or turned into corpses.

And me? A man going home his hair flecked with white.

The blue clouds, the mountain berries
black as beads of lacquer,
the mouse folding its paws together,
all elate me.

When I arrive the boy seeing his dad
turns his back and weeps.
His feet are dirty.
The two little girls are in the bedroom
in dresses cut and sewn so often that the flowers birds and sky
run together.

"How could I have forgotten
to bring you something?"
as I hand out silk, rouge and toys —
my wife's thin face begins to glow again.

In the morning our silly girls comb their hair
exactly like their mother's and make up their faces
in what we call the two-handed smear.

Yet I am sick; I have been vomiting at night.
And how do I bring up the subject of how to make a living?

after Tu Fu

A road, a bottle, the sky, a way of waiting
and it is upon me.

Nestled in the bottle,
mingled in the neck of the night,
it is thinner than blood
thinner than water
thinner, cooler than October sunlight.

Can you guess? Too tired?
It is as nameless as the good,
as elusive as evil.
If you whip it
it comes to love the whip.

Hurry, rush the gardens into bloom,
the war is still a range away.

All light dips under it
ignites it
and from him to her
from her to him
it circulates
and transmits
the secret
of the itch.

So my poems are always about it,
a time (like heaven's)
apart from hurt –
the procurement and the high,

the high, its emptiness,
the emptiness and the understanding
emptiness provides.

Its sweetness
its perfection
puffs up and swells up
and stings itself and
shriveling, dies
if there is no charity
if there is no touch.

from the Arabic

A long night of drinking wine
listening to the five musicians
seeing eyes flash from the corners.
A public man is open to ridicule
so I come to this place.
It is bad enough that my wife
knows me so well
but now the children too.

The first drink, raising the glass to my lips,
is itself a sexual act.
I have to drink to release the words and love.
I observe my mood swings throughout the night.

When she appears passing between the light and me
I imagine her red lips closing over me
but the gray already appears at the window,
I have waited too long.

Then it happens again, between the lamp and me
she walks, I watch!
And I see it is the moonlight
shining at the window.

Bending, she turns the lamp up
the sun seems to glow from her face
"Come to me friend
let us be one."

There is no mistaking now
the room is bright
and in the dawn she says
"Easy does it, not too quick
Come at me slow, I'll come with you."

from the Arabic

I rode five days as fast as I could
to see her again
and found she had gone with a merchant.

The flow of words came after the first drink.
By moonrise I was in love
with the possibility of love

. . . dodging the watch

Then,

in the heart of the quarter
from an alley without a name
a husky voice.

This is the first in Mozarabic.
I dedicate it to you, mindless lust,
the irreducible coal
that cool air from the alley fans into fire.

from the Mozarabic

Last night I went into the next county
and found a woman who was willing
rough red hair
and eyes that were hooded

The wind was blowing outside her house
where men lounged under the sycamores

I discovered the blend of corruption and innocence
I sought
There is an appeal
in cheap jewelry and mascara
that escapes the purist.

In the morning
we discover scratches
that testify to our love

The wind is died down,
it is a dry colorless day

my dear, did I tell you I am a Jew?

from the Hebrew

It is an ancient understanding,
a form of anesthesia,
that all rise skyward and live happily forever
and its opposite, equally believed
that we descend into fire
and suffer for eternity,
but the truth, told to me by seers,
is simpler and not ominous at all:
oblivion
and they repeat it,
no matter the joys of young flesh
and the dreams of the old:
oblivion
no matter the icicles in winter
or the irises in spring:
oblivion.

from the Hebrew

Were her fingers actually pudgy
or was that the wine?
We find happiness where we can
even in mock elegance
mock love

The night, the wind, the illusion:
all gone.
Left: dust and sunlight

I walk out of town,
slide down behind a stone wall
to hide from the wind.

from the Arabic

On a street corner
in the middle of the night
I put my tongue into your mouth

How do we dare?
We are separated by history and faith
and I, with a dwindling history
of love and rage

The darkness has a pulse
when I touch you there and there
and you rise to my touch

Later I run down the Street of Weights
breathing hard this poem.

from the Arabic

It is hard to say yes, a betrayal of all I cherish.

Yet yes – your face, my heart,
yes to long nights together
and sated, satisfy ourselves with one last kiss

or I can say no, close my eyes and say no
instead of eating, eaten,
just no, no to destiny,
no to rhetoric
for rhetoric – whether yes or no –
will not save me.

from the Arabic

Let's be objective
she had black nails
and black lips
and too much jewelry

but how I love dark hair

I was on Lemon St.
then in her room
then back on Lemon St
under the bright moon.

from the Arabic

They came by the house
They told us how it is going to be

No more death, no more pain
no old age, no babies

Have you seen my brothers?
Have you seen my sisters?

A rumble of storm:
horsemen of the sect
have vaporized
the people I love.

from the Hebrew

Testament

In this my 54th year
having had two parents
two wives, four children
loves, friendships,
having established my competence
in the world of keys
having been released by the authorities,
my mother having been twenty years in her ashes
and my father having decided to live forever,
having given away my possessions
shrunken my body and deadened my feelings,
it being that year
at five in the afternoon
the sun flashing through trees
the little pervert in me smiling
I leave you all.

My intention, to attend to particular
vulgar matters that concern you,
my will, to carry memories
from the hive to the page,
my desire to rise to the occasion
and dispose of the past,
my humor to write this testament
for all to read and understand.

To play the hypocrite is easy.
This next turn, three triple fearless twists
in air, with honey in my heart
light winking in my eye
poison on my lips,
I say goodbye to literature and love
goodbye to fatherhood and husbandry.

Now down to it
premature but timely,
let our displays begin
each our own carnival
with shining lights and thumping tubas,
an aria about me.

Wife one had rosy cheeks and Irish lips
and two chubby-cheeked Irish offspring
I loved the baby boy
with his blooming laugh
I loved the girl
and her griefs
Best of all I loved
the Irish mother
her fearless fears
her glowing face
and betrayed her with this list of six
        mother of ten
        whore in Juarez
        hippy chick
        clubfooted Margo
        half-Indian girl
        disembodied intellectual
and betray her here again
with black ink descending a cheap pen;
I would leave her irony
but that's reserved for people
with a sense of humor.

To you dear second wife
getting right to it
you already got it of course
I leave the house and land

that carry no debt
but ashes in the orchard
and this locket snapped open
to the two of us
in May, in love, in sunlight

What is left?
some poems?
In that case
to my singular friend
audience of one
I leave my poems
thirty years of trying to convey
the rhythm of a pail of water,
the way a woman lifts her hair up
off her neck
sorted into words
greasy rags in the corner
that ignite,
is it arson? accident?
the authority to prune them
but expressly not to add a word
deleting much, adding nothing
leaving bits of me, tiny mirrors

As for you the one from Meung
I leave you your good name
and fame

To you, mild voyeur, I bequest
the lust behind my seeing
photos, films, windows
framing women in their rooms
in shirts and slips

As for the eyes themselves
I leave them to the dog
he saw us clearly
Now let him see in color badly
instead of stars, clouds
let him learn to look into our hearts
not read our faces.
Too ironic for his species
he joined us as our equal
I withhold my tongue
his laughter was enough

my body to the air
it received 1000 pounds of it already
where they went, I go

the young
I leave them nothing
I have nothing that they need

I leave you this page
this poem an echo
of the shout I meant

I spoke twice. There is a boy here
and a child. I kill them
with this will and testament
and kill myself.
It is the year
I leave you all
and leave to you
the shifting light
that strikes the world.

after Villon

In the mid-1970s, realizing that I had not written anything of worth and giving up writing, I found that I missed the routine and translated Rimbaud's A Season In Hell. Although I had taken two years of French in high school and a year in college, I could barely read it. I depended on English translations by Fowlie, Schmidt, Peschel, Varese and others for the meaning, then put the poem into my English.

These are excerpts from the full translation.

A Season in Hell

Only recently, thinking I was about to give my last gasp, I looked for the key to that ancient celebration.

"God is love," I cried

And by that inspired remark, proved I was still hallucinating.

"You will always be a fool," mocks the demon who egged me on to my previous achievements. "Death is rewarded only to those who are genuinely selfish and evil."

Dear demon, I beg you, a less burning eye; and while you are waiting for my belated depravities, you who can appreciate a style stripped of adjectives and morals, let me present you with a few hideous pages from my notebook of hell.

I have the blue eyes and white eyes of my Gallic ancestors – their narrow heads and their clumsiness in battle. I think my clothes are as barbarous as theirs. I don't butter my hair though.

The Gauls were the most incompetent butchers and hay-burners of their time.

From them I have a love of heresy and sacrilege and vice – rage, lewdness, (heavenly lewdness), lying and laziness.

I have a horror of earning a living. Boss and worker are both peasants. "The pen is mightier than the plough." Everyone is expected to put his hand to something. A job leads to a family. Even beggars get to work on time. Petty crooks clock in and out. As for me, I'm still intact, so who cares.

But where did I get this treacherous tongue that talks me out of every duty? I never lift a hand, I'm idle as a toad, yet I've been everywhere, I know the best families of Europe, the families of liberated spirits, all the best bums and free-loaders.

I am on the coast of France. The lights from the town spread into the evening. I am quitting Europe. The sea air will corrode my lungs. Wasted climates will blacken my skin. I will swim, tramp fields, smoke, drink liquors hot as lava – like my ancestors around their fires.

And I will return with a gut of iron, leathered skin and convulsed eye. My face hardened like a mask will make people think I am of a strong race. I'll have gold. I'll be idle and brutal. Women nurse those fierce invalids home from hot countries. But now I am still an outcast. I loathe my country. For now, a drunken sleep on the beach.

In fact I am bored with boredom. I am tired of my rages and perversions and madness. I know the whims that end in disaster and I can do without them. Eschewing undue dizziness, let us evaluate the extent of my innocence.

I am no longer up to demanding the comfort of the whip. I no longer imagine I'm off on a honeymoon with J.C. for father-in-law.

Why should I be a product of logic? I say, God I want freedom and salvation. How should I go about it? No more kidding around. No more devotion and divine love. Each of us has his own logic, his own scorn, his own love. I choose to retain my spot at the top of the ladder of self-esteem.

As for happiness, domestic or not, no – I can't do it. I'm too dissipated. I know – work makes life fruitful – but my life is not weighty enough for that. It flies and floats above action, that quality so worshipped by the world.

What an old woman I've become, afraid to love death.

For a long time I claimed to possess all possible landscapes and I held in contempt the celebrities of modern painting and poetry.

I loved circus posters, old hotel signs, ads on trolley cars, erotic books devoid of grammar, old-fashioned novels, antique operas and inane songs.

I dreamed crusades, secret voyages of exploration, lands without histories, suffocating religious wars, a revolution of manners, the return of Atlantis – I believed in all marvels.

I invented the color of vowels. A was black, E white, I red, O blue, U green. I regulated the form and movement of each consonant and applauded myself for inventing a poetry of all the senses. I kept the copyrights of course.

I tried to express silence, the night, the inexpressible. I tried to capture frenzies, dizziness, madness and intoxication.

What to drink there
hidden by hazel thickets,
far from flocks and village girls
kneeling at the whirling water
in the long gold wink of afternoon.

What to drink in the young Oise
in the voiceless trees?

Give me golden liquors,
let me die

beneath the overcast
of sweating zinc.

The storm destroys the sky.
God's wind blows icicles
into the shining river.
The cold sands drink
the waters of the evening woods.
I weep. See gold. And cannot drink.

Four o'clock, a summer's morning,
still asleep in love's deep sea
the odors of the evening revelry
rising from the silent woods

and down beyond the trees
the carpenters in shirtsleeves
labor in the lumberyard.

As you can see, obsolete prosody played a large role in my "alchemy of the word."

I became good at hallucinating. When I looked at a factory I saw a mosque. A troop of boy scouts became angels. I saw locomotives in the sky, bedrooms at the bottom of a lake. I left my body. I saw the devil.

In the end I thought my confusions were sacred. I lay around inert and feverish envying caterpillars in the innocence of their limbo and moles in the virginity of their dark.

I became bitter and said goodbye to the world in all sorts of songs.

Let it come, let it come
the time of our delirium

I have waited wanting
to lose my fear and shame.

My blood runs sick
with thirst

That it come; let it come
the time of my delirium

I wait like a prairie
flowering with fodder

flourishing with the murmur
of obscene flies

oh may it come
my own delirium

I loved the desert, parched orchards, faded shops, wine mixed with warm water. I loitered in the stench of alleys and offered myself to the heat of the sun.

I cried "General, if any old cannons remain on what's left of your walls, bombard us with lumps of dried mud. Spatter the mirrors of the city. Rust the faucets."

Oh drunken fly in the tavern urinal, lover of borage, dissolved by a ray of sunlight.

I became a fabulous opera unto myself. I saw that all beings have a fatality for happiness. Action is not life but only a depreciation of some force, while morality is a feebleness of the brain.

It seemed to me that everyone has other lives. This gentleman does not suspect that he is also an angel. That family is a kennel of dogs. I've talked to men about their double lives. One of them, whom I loved, was a pig.

I didn't neglect a single sophistry of madness – madness under tight control. I can recite them all if you want. I know the system.

This new hour is very harsh, but I can say I have won. The gnashing of teeth, the hissing of fire, the reeking sighs abate. The filthy memories fade. And you beggars, thieves, friends of death, junkies of all sorts – you who are damned – should I avenge myself on you?

No. We must be absolutely modern.

No hymns. Hold the ground gained. The dried blood smokes on my face. I leave nothing behind except the horrible tree. A spiritual battle is as brutal as a battle of weapons. The vision of justice is God's pleasure alone.

This is a vigil. Let us welcome the influx of vigor and tenderness. At dawn, armed with ardent patience, we will enter magnificent cities.

What was I saying about a friendly hand? One fine advantage is that I can laugh at old lying loves and strike with shame those lying couples – I saw the hell of sex down there – and I shall be free to possess truth in a body united with soul.

*After translating A Season in Hell, I was not yet ready
to return to writing. I translated the Gilgamesh Epic. I read
a variety of translations but mine is taken primarily from the
literal word-by-word translation from the original tablets by
E. A. Speiser. I eliminated almost all of the repetition and
suppressed the names of innumerable gods. I used a basic
pentameter line, with much variation, except for the last section,
Death of Gilgamesh, which is written in the fragmentary form
which illustrates in what condition we have most of the epic.*

These are excerpts from the full translation.

From The Epic of Gilgamesh

[Gilgamesh is the king, Enkidu is a wild man who has been
domesticated.]

Enkidu walked in front, his woman walked behind him.
When they entered Uruk's market men stared and pushed
and said, "He's the spitting image of the king."
"He's stouter." "He's got more bone."
The men rejoiced and said, "Now Gilgamesh will meet his match,
now the dust will fly."

That night the bridal bed was made. The bride was ready for her husband.
But her husband waited in his father's house
and it was Gilgamesh who strode across the marketplace
and down the narrow street headed for her bed.
Then Enkidu rose up and blocked the way.
The king kept coming on but Enkidu stood fast.

They rammed like bulls and threw each other back and forth
and shattered gateposts and shook the earthen walls
and breathed like horses after racing.
Then Gilgamesh set his feet, bent his knee
and threw the wild man to the street.
The fight was over, their fury ended.
Enkidu stood and said, "You are better, Gilgamesh,
your mother gave you strength and god-the-wind has made you king."
And they were glad, they embraced and they were friends.

When Gilgamesh washed his long soft hair and cleaned his weapons
and chose new robes and put on his crown,
Ishtar the goddess raised an eye at his beauty
saying "Gilgamesh, come, and be my husband,
I will make a chariot of gold for you

and I will be the one who bears your seed."

"Great Ishtar, if I became your husband
what gifts could I, a mortal, give to you, a goddess?
Gods need neither food nor drink.
What oils or clothes could I, grounded in the earth,
give to you a queen of beauty?
And also, to be truthful, if we were married
I cannot help but wonder what my fate would be.
Your lovers find you are a fire died down in the dawn,
a broken door that lets the wind blow through.
Name a man who lived to praise you.
There was Tammuz, lover of your youth:
you changed him to a many-colored pigeon
and then struck him, broke his wing.
Now he sits in the morning grove and cries "My wing, my wing."
You loved the lion and dug seven pits for him,

the stallion and bestowed upon him whip and spur
and now he runs for men and muddies water when he drinks;
then the shepherd, the one who prepared cakes of meal
and slaughtered kids for you,
him you struck and changed into a wolf
and now the other shepherds drive him off,
his own hounds track him.
There was Ishullam, your father's gardener,
who gave you raisin cakes and dates and daily bread
for all your family,
you made eyes at him to come
and he simple soul had the nerve to say
"what do you want with me?
My wife has baked and I have eaten."
For that, he got to be the mole that lives beneath the soil.
Now tell me, am I to take you in my arms?"

The goddess was enraged and went before her father
Anu, lord of all the gods, and said
"My father, greatest single god,
Gilgamesh the king of Uruk
has insulted me by telling every tale of misplaced love I ever had,
then using them to turn me down."
"But Ishtar, daughter, surely you invited this?"
"My father, what I want is, please create a bull of heaven for me."
But Anu said: "When I make a bull of heaven
seven years of drought and famine follow."
Ishtar answered: "I know that and have gathered grain and grass
enough to last full seven years.

O father, if you don't I will enter hell and break the bolts off
and swing the doors wide and raise the dead to earth, alive and eating."
So Anu created a bull of heaven for his daughter Ishtar
and it fell to earth and with a single thrust slew a hundred men,
with another thrust a hundred more, it slew five hundred men.

With its sixth, it slew a hundred more.
With its tenth, it sprang at Enkidu who slipped aside.
It charged again and Enkidu leapt up, seized its horns
and swung himself head first past the shining horns
so close that foam flicked his face, the thick tail brushed his side.
He called to Gilgamesh, "My friend, we have boasted
that our names will live in fame. Let us now ensure it."
They thrust their swords between the neck and shoulder,
first Enkidu then Gilgamesh thrust his sword
deep between neck and shoulder until the great bull finally fell.

Ishtar saw it all. She sprang to the walls of Uruk
and cried a curse: "Woe to Gilgamesh. Woe to Enkidu.
They have slain the bull of heaven and insulted me."
Enkidu looked up, saw the goddess on the walls
calling misery down on them
and tore a thigh from the carcass of the bull and tossed it to her.
"If I could catch you goddess, I would lash the entrails to your hide."
The goddess summoned all the priests and temple prostitutes
and set them wailing.
Gilgamesh called the armorers and artisans to admire
the thickness of the horns that held six measures each of oil
and were plated two fingers thick with lapis lazuli.
He took the horns and hung them in his palace.
Then the brothers washed their hands in the river called Euphrates
and rode through Uruk in their gold and gleaming chariot
and people gathered gazing on them and crying
"Who is, who is the most splendid of men?"
and the surging girls crying back
"Gilgamesh is the most glorious of heroes."

Enkidu and Gilgamesh lay down to sleep
and it was Enkidu who rose in the middle of the night
to tell his friend his dream.

"I dreamed," he mumbled half asleep
"Why are the gods in council?"
and stumbled back to bed.
The next night, he dreamed again.
"The heavens moaned and the earth moaned in reply.
I stood before an awful thing whose face was dark as storm clouds,
its talons sharp as eagle's. It leapt upon me
overpowered me and pushed me under.
Then it led me down the road that goes one way
to the house which no one leaves,
the people there live deprived of light, their meat is dirt,
their meal is clay and they are clothed like birds with wings for garments.
In the house of dust I saw kings lay aside their crowns and work like slaves
I saw princes born to luxury toll in numbing labor
I saw the priests of incantation and the priests of ecstasy
I saw the king of Kish whose eagle carried him to heaven
I saw the god of cattle
I saw the queen of darkness
and her scribe called Belit-Sheri squatting in the dust
marking in the book of death
and when she raised her head and looked at me I woke afraid
like a man wandering in the waste of the rushes
or a man seized by the royal police,
my heart pounding with terror.
My brother, please, not me,
let it be someone else's name on that tablet."

Death of Gilgamesh
A literal transcription from tablet

Gilgamesh (the) son of Nissum
his beloved wife his son
The wife, his beloved concubine
his musicians beloved chief valet
the palace attendants
>   I have seen
>   weeps over (it)
>   I have seen
>   eats bread
>   I have seen
>   drinks water

like that of a god
>   he enters the palace

>   hast thou seen
>   like a beautiful standard

Him who fell down from the mast

the pegs pulled out

Him who died a sudden death
>   hast thou seen

He lies upon the night couch and drinks pure water
Him who was killed in battle
>   corpse down the river

His spirit finds no
        rest in the underworld

Gilgamesh (the) son of Nissum
made heavy
Gilgamesh
which he interpreted to them
they answer
why dost thy cry?
Why has it been made?

he brought forth
there is not
strength, firm muscle
escaped not the hand

looked upon
        the
        seized.

Ibn Hazm[1] writes to his nephew
(adapted from The Ring of the Dove)[2]

To answer your question,
it was a slave girl who taught me what exile means.
Born in our house on the eastside[3]
when our family still cast a shadow on the land,
(my father was vizier and advisor to the court)[4]
she and I grew up together, she one year older
flittering about the mansion like a bird which can't find a window

until at sixteen she became reserved and modest,
not winking and sighing like the other girls
and a beauty, a blond with brown eyes, her lashes shone,
her face like mother of pearl, her figure slender as a sapling,
while she went about her chores
the way the moon crosses the sky.
We barely spoke and when we did,
only banal words about the weather,
(even then, her voice a cooing dove).
She was afraid of men, even me, whose love was pure,
the product of the poetry then in vogue.
I was too young to understand
why she would resist our love.
Although we never touched or kissed she touched my soul.

Two years I loved her bluish veil,
brocaded blouse and tiny slippers.
It made no difference. She left my letters where they lay,
their ink diluted with my tears.
When I approached she flew, a quail flushed from high grass

and in desperation I moved away to the west side[5]
to study the Koran, calligraphy and literature.

Then trouble, as you know: war[6] and with it,
surveillance, slander, crushing fines, assaults and jail.
These broke my father and he died,
(God have mercy on his soul).[7]
At the funeral I saw her with the other women
weeping and wailing, lovelier than ever,
tears like pearls splashing down her front.
My puppy love was gone replaced by passion,
the fire smoldering in my heart
was fanned by grief and blazed.
That night, consumed by love and sorrow,
I wrote my first poem:

> They weep for one who's dead
> high-honored in his tomb.
> Their tears are better shed
> for me who lives in gloom.
> O wonder that they sigh
> for him who lies at rest
> yet mourn not me who dies
> most cruelly sad, oppressed.

When the Berbers sacked our city we were banned;
I moved north[8] where life passed like a dream
dreamed just before dawn.
I forgot her!

After six long years I returned[9]
and met a woman whom I did not recognize,
her loveliness was gone, her luster faded,
like Córdoba itself a trampled garden, a polluted spring,
her eyes no longer gleamed but were dull and sunken

in her face which now was but a mask of scorn
for the men of the household
and what she was obliged to do for them.

And my youth, my love, my city were over
and I began a life of wandering and exile
seeking consolation in philosophy and poetry.

What I learned in exile?
Be bold in love, embrace the moment with the girl,
because life doesn't stop, it flows forward
and consists of incessant change.
Time requires something of us
but what, we don't know and won't know
until it is too late.

If there is blame, it is mine for leaving and forgetting.

1. Abū Muḥammad ʿAlī ibn Aḥmad ibn Saʿīd ibn Ḥazm (Arabic: أبو
محمد علي بن احمد بن سعيد بن حزم); also sometimes known as al-
Andalusī aẓ-Ẓāhirī; 994 –1064 a.d., was an Andalusian polymath
born in Córdoba.

2. *The Ring of the Dove* (Arabic: طوق الحمامة, *Ṭawq al-Ḥamāmah*[) is
a treatise on love written ca. 1027. A. R. Nykl of the Oriental
Institute of Chicago translated the work, publishing in 1931, and A.
J. Arberry's translation was published in 1951. This poem is adapted
from Arberry's translation.

3. The eastside quarter of Córdoba was called Rabad al-Zahira.

4. Ibn Hazm's father held a high advisory position in the court of Caliph
Hisham II, and Ibn Hazm himself entered service as vizier to Abd al-
Rahman V al Mustazhir.

5. Córdoba's westside was called Balat Mughith.

6. War between Umayyads, the ruling Arab family of Andalusia, and
Hammudids, a Berber dynastic that briefly ruled the Caliphate of
Córdoba and the taifas of Malaga and Algeciras.

7. The poet's father died June 12, 1012, when Ibn Hazm was 8 years old.

8. Ibn Hazm lived at various times in Almeria, Aznalcazar and Valencia.

9. Ibn Hazm returned to Córdoba in 1019, age 25. It is believed that he
was living in Jativa when he wrote "The Ring of the Dove" at the age
of 33.

"It is written"
and I wrote it
in the flashing light.
I wrote it in one shot
over a lifetime.

ABOUT THE AUTHOR

Born into a secular Jewish family in Chicago in 1940, Jim Levy moved with his parents Kay and Norman Levy and older sister Katherine to Los Angeles in 1945. His father, who had spent three years serving in WWII as a psychiatrist, opened a practice in Beverly Hills as a Freudian psychoanalyst. Jim grew up surrounded by his parents' friends: artists, writers and eccentrics on his mother's side, Hollywood people and doctors on his father's. His younger sister Mary was born in 1947.

During the late 1940s and early 1950s, Levy's mother took the three children to spend the summers in Taos, New Mexico. Her landlady was Mabel Dodge Luhan and she became friends with the people who had been in the D. H. Lawrence circle. The summers in Taos gave Levy a life-long love of the landscape and cultures of northern New Mexico.

Levy attended public schools until age thirteen and then spent four years at The Thacher School in Ojai, California, where he met his life-long friend Harvey Mudd. They received a grounding in American and British literature, history, Latin, French and the sciences and math. While at boarding school, his main interests were girls and sports. He earned nine varsity letters in soccer, basketball and track, was named all-conference in the three sports, and went to the California interscholastic quarterfinals in the mile, coming in fourth at 4:47:2.

For five summers, Levy worked jobs at Sunkist Corp. in downtown L.A. and at a factory in Burbank. On a break in August, 1955, when he and his father were traveling through New Mexico and Arizona, he was one of the few non-Native Americans, perhaps the first, to run in the long-distance Hopi race associated with the Snake Dance. He came in last, beaten by middle-aged men and pre-teens.

Expected to go to Princeton where his grandfather, uncle and father had gone, he instead chose Pomona College, where he played freshman basketball and broke the freshman scoring record. He played varsity basketball for a year and then focused his time on music and literature. Influenced by the Beats, he rode freight trains up and down California and hitchhiked in Mexico and the Southwest. After reading Rimbaud's *Illuminations,* he began writing poetry.

At the age of twenty, Levy and Mudd spent a year abroad, Levy mostly in a small village south of Rome, Mudd in Cordova, Toledo and the Middle East. Returning in 1962, Levy enrolled at U.C. Berkeley during the Free Speech era, although he played no part in it. He earned his B.A. in English and History and a certificate in secondary teaching.

While at Berkeley, Levy met and began an affair with Deirdre Blomfield-Brown, who had two children and was married to a wealthy man. They started to live together with her two children in 1965 and married in 1966, working as caretakers of a ranch in Sonoma. In 1968 they moved to Ajijic, Mexico and became involved with the drop-out crowd smoking hashish and taking LSD and other hallucinogenic drugs. A year later they moved to Arroyo Hondo, New Mexico. Levy became the editor of a counter-culture magazine called *The Fountain of Light.*

The marriage ended in 1971. Levy took the Basque freighter Mar Egeo to Valencia and drifted through Spain and Morocco. He lived for a month on the southern coast of Ghana, where he contracted a serious case of malaria, and he spent more months in Nairobi and on the island of Lamu off the coast of Kenya. From there, he went to Ethiopia and stayed ten days in Harar, where Rimbaud had been a trader. He recovered from malaria and intestinal diseases in Israel and in Montainville, France with his older sister.

In 1972 Levy began living in Arroyo Hondo, New Mexico with Phaedra Greenwood, a writer with an infant son named Alexander. They had a daughter Sara in 1974 and were married in 1977. His mother Kay, whose love of literature had inspired his own, died in March, 1975 at the age of 66, an event which had a profound effect on the rest of his life.

Levy stayed in touch with his first wife, Deirdre, who changed her name to Pema Chödrön, became a Tibetan Buddhist nun in 1974 and received full ordination in 1984. Pema became a teacher and began publishing edited transcripts of her talks. *When Things Fall Apart, The Wisdom of No Escape* and her other books and audios have become increasingly popular.

During the 1960s, Levy wrote poetry and four novels, all of which he destroyed when he and his wife Deirdre separated. During most of the 1970s, he wrote by day and worked by night as janitor, projectionist, or manager at the Taos Plaza Theater. In 1978 he became executive director of the Harwood Foundation of the University of New Mexico, a public library and cultural center. This became what was to be a thirty-five year career working for nonprofit organizations.

In 1985 he again destroyed most of what he had written, although some poems survived in letters and journals. He and Phaedra took their children on a five-month trip to Europe, each with one backpack, to Spain, Sicily, Italy, Switzerland, France, England and Scotland. Upon returning they lived in Carrboro, North Carolina for three years, where Levy had a detached retina in his right eye and after four operations, lost the sight in that eye. He had preventive surgery on the retina in his left eye, which degraded his vision in that eye.

In 1989, they moved to Boulder, Colorado, where Levy worked as a senior staff member at the Housing Authority of the City of Boulder. He and Phaedra separated in 1992 and were divorced in 1994.

For several years, Levy lived an unsettled life, living in Pátzcuaro, Mexico, Montreal, Spain, and California. He returned to Taos in 1999, working as a consultant to nonprofit organizations. After surviving a period of serious depression, he joined a men's support group which continues to the present. He and Phaedra were reunited in 2003 in the house in Arroyo Hondo, where they continue to write books. Phaedra published *Beside The Rio Hondo* and *North with the Spring,* and edited and co-authored *Drinking from the Stream.* Their son Alexander lives in the Bay Area as a videographer and their daughter Sara lives in Denver as a senior manager with Whole Foods Market.

After a lifetime of destroying his works and declining to publish, Levy decided at age 74 to begin publishing what remained of his writing. He published *Corazón (and Merkle)*, a book about his two dogs, and *Cooler Than October Sunlight,* his selected poems. In 2015, The Porcupine Press is publishing *The Poems of Caius Herennius Felix,* a fictitious first-century Roman Spanish poet, and *Joy To Come,* a collection of essays. In 2016 he will publish his memoirs and a short book of aphorisms and meditations.

Jim Levy can be reached at 575 776-5763, jim@start-nonprofit.com and at P.O. Box 282, Arroyo Hondo, NM 87513.